Bisclavret

A Medieval Werewolf Tale with Original Text, Translations, and Word Lists

Translated by
Matthew Leigh Embleton

Copyright ©2025 Matthew Leigh Embleton. All rights reserved.

Bisclavret

Bisclavret 4
Word List *(Old French to English)* 21
Word List *(English to Old French)* 38

Cover: Old French text over an outline of France. Author's design.

The original Old French text is in the public domain.
This translation ©2021 Matthew Leigh Embleton
©2025 Matthew Leigh Embleton (This Edition)

Acknowledgments

I have long been fascinated by languages and history, and I am very grateful to the special people in my life who have supported and encouraged me in my work. Thank you for believing in me. You know who you are.

Introduction

Marie de France (fl 1160 to 1215) was a poet born in France who lived in England during the late 12th century. She was well known at the Plantagenet royal court of King Henry II of England and Eleanor of Aquitaine, and she is believed to have been an abbess of a monastery. Her poems or 'Lais' are believed to have been written sometime between 1160 and 1175 drawing upon Breton and Arthurian myths and legends.

It is written in a form of Old French known as 'Anglo-Norman', which came from 'Old Norman', part of the 'Langues d'oïl' dialect continuum of Gallo-Romance languages. Old French is the result of a gradual separation from Vulgar Latin and Common Romance, coming into contact with influences from Gaulish (Continental Celtic), and Frankish (Germanic).

The text is presented in the original Old French, with a literal word-for-word line-by-line translation, and a Modern English translation, all side-by-side. In this way, it is possible to see and feel how Old French worked and how it has evolved.

Also included is a word list with 1,318 Old French words translated in to English, and 1,271 English words translated into Old French.

This book is designed to be of use and interest to anyone with a passion for the Old French language, French history, or languages and history in general.

Marie de France - Bisclavret

Bisclavret

	Old French	Literal	English
1	Quant des lais faire m'entremet,	When of-them lays do I-begin,	When I begin (to compose) lays,
2	ne vueil ubliër Bisclavret.	not I-wish forget Bisclavret.	I do not wish to forget Bisclavret.
3	Bisclavret a nun en Bretan,	Bisclavret has the-name in Breton,	His name is Bisclavret in Breton,
4	Garulf l'apelent li Norman.	Garulf they-call the Normans.	The Normans call him Garulf.
5	Jadis le poeit hum oïr	Days-passed one could him hear	In days passed one could hear him,
6	e sovent suleit avenir,	and time-to-time used frequently,	and this used to happen frequently,
7	hume plusur garulf devindrent	man many Garulf became	many a man became a werewolf
8	e es boscages maisun tindrent.	and in-those woods house had.	and made his house in the woods.
9	Garulf, ceo est beste salvage;	Garulf, behold-this is beast savage;	Werewolf, that is a wild animal;
10	tant cum il est en cele rage,	as-much with it is in this rage,	as long as he is in this rage,
11	humes devure, grant mal fait;	men devours, great harm does;	He devours men, and does great harm;
12	es granz forez converse e vait.	in-those grand forests about and goes.	In the grand forests he goes about.
13	Cest afaire les ore ester;	This matter let now stand;	This matter now I let be;
14	del Bisclavret vus vueil cunter.	of-this Bisclavret you I-want to-recount.	I want to tell you about Bisclavret.
15	En Bretaigne maneit uns ber,	In Brittany lived one baron,	In Brittany there lived a baron,
16	merveille l'ai oï loër.	marvellously of-him I-hear praise.	of whom I hear marvellous praise.
17	Beals chevaliers e bons esteit	Handsome knight and good he-was	A handsome and good knight he was,
18	e noblement se cunteneit.	and nobly he led-himself.	And nobly he led himself.

Marie de France - Bisclavret

	Old French	Literal	English
19	*De sun seignur esteit privez*	Of his lord he-was close	Of his lord he was a close friend,
20	*e de tuz ses veisins amez.*	and of all his neighbours loved.	and by all his neighbours he was loved.
21	*Femme ot espuse mult vaillant*	Woman had wife much valiant	He had a woman as his wife who was much valiant,
22	*e ki mult faiseit bel semblant.*	and of much made beautiful appearance.	and who was beautiful in appearance.
23	*Il amot li e ele lui;*	He loved her and she him;	He loved her, and she loved him;
24	*mes d'une chose ert grant ennui,*	but of-one thing was great grief,	but one thing caused her great grief,
25	*qu'en la semeine le perdeit*	that-in the week him lost	that in the week she lost him,
26	*treis jurs entiers qu'el ne saveit*	three days entire with not knowing	for three days without knowing,
27	*que deveneit ne u alout,*	what became nor where went,	what became of him nor where he went,
28	*ne nuls des soens niënt n'en sout.*	nor none of his nothing about knew.	and none of his people knew about it.
29	*Une feiz esteit repairiez*	One time was-he returned	Once he returned
30	*a sa maisun joius e liez;*	to his home joyous and happy;	to his home joyous and happy;
31	*demandé li a e enquis.*	asked she to and inquired.	she asked and inquired.
32	*Sire', fait el, bealz, dulz amis,*	'My-lord', said she, 'gentle, sweet friend,	'My lord', she said, 'gentle and sweet friend,
33	*une chose vus demandasse*	one thing I-wish to-ask	one thing I wish to ask you
34	*mult volentiers, se jeo osasse;*	much willing, if I dare;	very much, if I dare;
35	*mes jeo criem tant vostre curut*	but I fear so-much your anger	but I fear your anger so much
36	*que nule rien tant ne redut'.*	that any nothing as-much nor dread'.	that there is nothing I dread so much'.
37	*Quant il l'oï, si l'acola,*	When he that-heard, so he-embraced,	When he heard that, he embraced her,

Marie de France - Bisclavret

	Old French	Literal	English
38	vers lui la traist, si la baisa.	to him her drew-close, so her kissed.	drew her close to him, and kissed her.
39	Dame', fait il, or demandez!	'Madam', said he, 'just ask!	'Madam', he said, 'just ask!
40	Ja cele chose ne querrez,	Never such thing not ask,	Never such a thing will you ask,
41	se jo la sai, ne la vus die'.	of me that I-know, not the answer you.	of me that if I know, I will not answer you.
42	Par fei', fet ele, or sui guarie!	By faith, said she, 'now I-am relieved!	'By my faith', she said, 'now I am relieved!'
43	Sire, jeo sui en tel esfrei	My-lord, I am in much fear	My lord, I am in such fear,
44	les jurs quant vus partez de mei.	the days when you part from me.	on the days when you take leave of me.
45	El cuer en ai mult grant dolur	In my-heart in have much great pain	In my heart I have such great pain,
46	e de vus perdre tel poür,	and of you loss such horror,	and such horror at the thought of losing you,
47	se jeo nen ai hastif cunfort,	if I do-not have swift comfort,	that if I do not have swift comfort,
48	bien tost en puis aveir la mort.	well quickly and then have of death.	then I may well die soon.
49	Kar me dites u vus alez,	Come me tell where you go,	Come now, tell me where you go,
50	u vus estes e conversez!	where you are and about!	where you are, and where you dwell!
51	Mun esciënt que vus amez,	To-me it-seems that you-have a-love,	It seems to me as though you have a sweetheart,
52	e se si est, vus meserrez'.	and if so are, you misguided'.	and if so, you are misguided'.
53	Dame', fet il, pur deu merci!	'Madam', said he, by god's mercy!	'Madam', he said, 'by god's mercy!
54	Mals m'en vendra, se jol vus di;	Bad to-me comes, if I you tell;	Bad will come to me, if I tell you;
55	kar de m'amur vus partirai	therefore of my-love yours will-part	therefore my love will part,
56	e mei meïsmes en perdrai'.	and me myself then destroy.	and then me myself will be destroyed.

Marie de France - Bisclavret

	Old French	Literal	English
57	*Quant la dame l'a entendu,*	When the lady this heard,	When the lady heard this,
58	*ne l'a niënt en gab tenu.*	nor that nothing in jest beheld.	she knew that it was not in jest.
59	*Suventes feiz li demanda.*	Repeatedly put she questions.	Repeatedly she asked him questions.
60	*Tant le blandi e losenja*	So-much him cajoled and praised	So she flattered and praised him,
61	*que s'aventure li cunta;*	that his-adventure he recounted;	that he told her of his adventure;
62	*nule chose ne li cela.*	any thing not was concealed.	and nothing did he conceal from her.
63	*Dame, jeo deviene bisclavret.*	Madam, I become Bisclavret.	Madam, I become a werewolf.
64	*En cele grant forest me met*	In that great forest I go	In that great forest I go,
65	*al plus espés de la gualdine,*	to most thick of the forest,	to the thickest part of the woods,
66	*s'i vif de preie e de ravine'.*	thus live by plunder and of theft.	and there I live by plunder and theft.
67	*Quant il li aveit tut cunté,*	When he her had all recounted,	When he had recounted everything to her,
68	*enquis li a e demandé*	queried she and of asked	she queried him and asked him
69	*s'il se despueille u vet vestuz.*	whether he unclothed or goes dressed.	whether he went clothed or unclothed.
70	*Dame', fet il, jeo vois tuz nuz'.*	Madam', said he, 'I go totally nude'.	Madam', he said, 'I go totally naked'.
71	*Di mei pur deu u sunt voz dras!'*	'Tell me by god where are your clothes!'	'Tell me by god where are your clothes!'
72	*Dame, ceo ne dirai jeo pas;*	'Madam, this not will-tell I not;	'Madam, this I do not want to tell you;
73	*kar se jes eüsse perduz*	because if I were to-lose	because if I were to lose them,
74	*e de ceo fusse aparceüz,*	and of that had-been aware,	and if I become aware (of losing them),
75	*bisclavret sereie a tuz jurs.*	Bisclavret I-would-be of all days.	I would be a werewolf for all days.
76	*Ja nen avreie mes sucurs,*	I not could me help,	No help could ever again avail me,
77	*desi qu'il me fussent rendu.*	until which to-me would-be returned.	until they would be returned to me.

Marie de France - Bisclavret

	Old French	Literal	English
78	Pur ceo ne vueil qu'il seit seü'.	Therefore this not want which to-be known.	Therefore that is why I do not wish it to be known.
79	Sire', la dame li respunt,	'My-lord', the woman to-him responded,	'My lord', the woman responded to him,
80	jeo vus eim plus que tut le mund.	'I you love more than all the world.	'I love you more than all the world.
81	Nel me devez nïent celer	Not me should nothing conceal	Nothing should you conceal from me,
82	ne mei de nule rien duter;	nor mine of any nothing doubt;	Nor doubt my understanding of anything;
83	ne semblereit pas amistié,	not would-look-like not friendship,	that would not look like friendship,
84	Qu'ai jeo forfait, pur quel pechié	what-have I committed, by what sin	what have I committed, and by what sin
85	me dutez vus de nule rien?	me doubt you of not nothing?	that you doubt me not of nothing?
86	Dites le mei! Si ferez bien'.	Tell it to-me! So will-do well.	Tell me, so you will do well.
87	Tant l'anguissa, tant le suzprist,	So anguish, such he under-pressed,	Such anguish, he was pressed,
88	ne pout el faire, si li dist.	naught could he do, but her tell.	there was naught he could do but tell her.
89	Dame', fet il, de lez cel bois,	'Madam', said he, 'of near the forest,	Madam', he said, 'near the forest,
90	lez le chemin par unt jeo vois,	near the path by then I go,	near the path I go by,
91	une viez chapele i estait,	an old chapel is standing,	there stands an old chapel,
92	ki meinte feiz grant bien me fait.	which many times great good me has-done.	which many times has done me well.
93	La est la piere cruese e lee	There is the stone hollow and wide	There is a hollow and wide stone
94	suz un buissun, dedenz cavee.	under a bush, inside dug-out.	under a bush, inside a dug-out.
95	Mes dras i met suz le buissun,	My clothes I put under the bush,	I put my clothes under the bush,
96	tant que jeo revienc a maisun'.	until that I return to home.	until I return home.

Marie de France - Bisclavret

	Old French	Literal	English
97	La dame oï cele merveille,	The lady heard this marvel,	The lady heard this marvel,
98	de poür fu tute vermeille.	with fear became all crimson.	and became crimson with fear.
99	De l'aventure s'esfrea.	By the-event she-was-terrified.	By the event she was terrified.
100	En maint endreit se purpensa	In many ways she purposed	In many ways she thought,
101	cum ele s'en peüst partir;	how she if could part-with;	how she could part with him;
102	ne voleit mes lez lui gisir.	no-longer wanted with near him to-lie.	no longer did she want to lie near him.
103	Un chevalier de la cuntree,	A knight from the country,	A knight from the country,
104	ki lungement l'aveit amee	which long her-had loved	Who had long loved her
105	e mult preiee e mult requise	and much courted and much desired	and much courted and desired her
106	e mult duné en sun servise,	and much dedicated to her service,	and was much dedicated to her service,
107	(ele ne l'aveit unc amé	(she not him-had never loved	(she had never loved him,
108	ne de s'amur aseüré),	nor of love assured),	nor assured him of her love),
109	celui manda par sun message,	for-him sent-for by a message,	she sent for him by message,
110	si li descovri sun curage.	and to-him revealed her heart.	and revealed her sentiments to him.
111	Amis', fet ele, seiez liez!	'Friend', said she, 'be happy!	Friend', she said, 'be happy!
112	Ceo dunt vus estes travailliez	That which you are striving	That what you have been striving for
113	vus otrei jeo senz nul respit;	you grant I without any delay;	I grant you without any delay;
114	ja n'i avrez nul cuntredit.	never none will have any opposition.	you will never have any opposition.
115	M'amur e mun cors vus otrei:	my-love and my body yours grant:	My love and my body I grant you:

Marie de France - Bisclavret

	Old French	Literal	English
116	*vostre drue faites de mei!'*	your mistress make of me!'	make me your mistress!'
117	*Cil l'en mercie bonement*	This-he her thanks very-well	For this he thanks her very well
118	*e la fiance de li prent,*	and her promise of he receives,	and he receives her promise,
119	*e el le met a sairement.*	and she him puts under oath.	and she puts him under oath.
120	*Puis li cunta cumfaitement*	Then she recounted in-such-way	Then she told him which way
121	*sis sire ala e qu'il devint.*	her husband went and what became.	her husband went and what became of him.
122	*Tute la veie que il tint*	All the way that he travelled	The whole way that he travelled
123	*vers la forest li enseigna;*	to the forest she indicated;	to the forest she indicated;
124	*pur sa despueille l'enveia.*	for his clothes she-sent-for.	she sent him for her husband's clothes.
125	*Issi fu Bisclavret traïz*	Thus was Bisclavret betrayed	Thus was Bisclavret betrayed
126	*e par sa femme mal bailliz.*	and by this woman badly treated.	and treated badly by this woman.
127	*Pur ceo qu'um le perdeit sovent,*	Because that of-him one missed frequently,	Because he was frequently absent,
128	*quidouent tuit comunalment*	thought-they all together	they all thought together,
129	*que dunc s'en fust del tut alez.*	that so it was of all gone.	that he had gone for good.
130	*Asez fu quis e demandez:*	Much was he of sought-for:	Much was he sought and hunted for:
131	*mes n'en porent mie trover,*	but not could-they not-at-all find,	But they could not at all find him,
132	*si lur estut laissier ester.*	so let stand left was.	and so it was let be.
133	*La dame a cil dunc espusee,*	The woman then him so married,	The woman then married the one,
134	*que lungement aveit amee.*	who long had loved.	who had long lover her.

Marie de France - Bisclavret

	Old French	Literal	English
135	*Issi remest un an entier,*	So remained one year entire,	So remained a whole year,
136	*tant que li reis ala chacier.*	until that the king of-the hunt.	until the king joined the hunt.
137	*A la forest ala tut dreit*	To the forest of all straight	to the forest his way led straight
138	*la u li Bisclavret esteit.*	there where he Bisclavret stayed.	there where the were Bisclavret stayed.
139	*Quant li chien furent descuplé,*	When the dogs were released,	When the dogs were released,
140	*le Bisclavret unt encuntré.*	the Bisclavret they encountered.	they encountered Bisclavret.
141	*A lui cururent tutejur*	Of him chased all-the-day	They chased him all day
142	*e li chien e li veneür,*	and the dogs and the hunters,	and the dogs and hunters,
143	*tant que pur poi ne l'ourent pris*	until which all but not caught prize	all but caught him
144	*e tut deciré e mal mis.*	and all tear and badly treated.	and all but tore and ripped him.
145	*Des que il a le rei choisi,*	Of when he of the king saw,	And when he saw the king,
146	*vers lui curut querre merci.*	went he running asking-for mercy.	He went running asking for mercy.
147	*Il l'aveit pris par sun estrié,*	He had seized by his stirrup,	He seized him by his stirrup,
148	*la jambe li baise e le pié.*	his leg he kisses and his feet.	kissed his legs and feet.
149	*Li reis le vit, grant poür a;*	The king him saw, great fear had;	When the king saw him, he had great fear;
150	*ses cumpaignuns tuz apela.*	his companions all he-called.	he called all his companions.
151	*Seignur', fet il, avant venez!*	'Sires', said he, 'forward come!	'Sires', he said, 'come forward!
152	*Iceste merveille esguardez,*	This marvel look-at,	Look at this marvel,
153	*cum ceste beste s'umilie!*	how this beast is-humbled!	how the beast is humbled!

Marie de France - Bisclavret

	Old French	Literal	English
154	*Ele a sen d'ume, merci crie.*	He has sense of-a-man, mercy asks-for.	He has the sense of a man, who asks for mercy.
155	*Chaciez mei tuz cez chiens ariere,*	Chase from-me all these dogs back,	Chase from me all these dogs back,
156	*si guardez que hum ne la fiere!*	and take-care that he not is hit!	and take care that he is not hit!.
157	*Ceste beste a entente e sen.*	This beast has reason and sense.	This beast has reason and sense.
158	*Espleitiez vus! Alum nus en!*	Hurry you! Let-us we go!	Hurry! Let us all go!
159	*A la beste durrai ma pes:*	To the beast grant my peace:	To the beast grant my peace:
160	*kar jeo ne chacerai hui mes'.*	because I not will-hunt this-day furthermore.	Because from this day I do not wish to hunt any more.
161	*Li reis s'en est turnez a tant.*	The king then was returned at such-time.	The king then returned after a time.
162	*Li Bisclavret le vet siwant;*	The Bisclavret him there followed;	The Bisclavret followed him there;
163	*mult se tint pres, n'en volt partir,*	much he travels close, nor wants to-part,	he travels close to him, not wanting to leave him,
164	*il n'a cure de lui guerpir,*	he not-has care of him abandoning,	taking care not to abandon him,
165	*Li reis l'en meine en sun chastel.*	The king him takes to his castle.	The king takes him to his castle.
166	*Mult en fu liez, mult li est bel,*	Very he is happy, much he is well,	He is very happy, and very much well,
167	*kar unkes mes tel n'ot veü;*	because never he has before seen;	because he has never seen before;
168	*a grant merveille l'ot tenu*	a great wonder before beheld	a great wonder before beheld
169	*e mult le tint a grant chierté.*	and much him held of great fondness.	and he held him in great fondness.
170	*A tuz les suens a comandé*	Of all his people he commanded	Of all his people he commanded
171	*que sur s'amur le guardent bien*	for sure for-the-love-of him guard well	for the king's sake to guard him well
172	*e ne li mesfacent de rien,*	and not him harm of any,	and cause him no harm,

Marie de France - Bisclavret

	Old French	Literal	English
173	*ne par nul d'els ne seit feruz;*	nor by anyone be he to-be beaten;	nor be beaten by anyone;
174	*bien seit abevrez e peüz.*	well to-be drink and food.	to be given drink and food.
175	*Cil le guarderent volentiers*	They him guarded gladly	They guarded him gladly.
176	*tuz jurs entre les chevaliers,*	all days among the knights,	All days he was among the knights,
177	*e pres del rei s'alout culchier.*	and close to the-king next-to slept.	And next to the king he slept.
178	*N'i a celui ki ne l'ait chier;*	No-one is who-him that not has love;	There is no one who does not love him;
179	*tant esteit frans e de bon aire:*	so noble engaging and of good appearance:	so noble engaging and of good appearance:
180	*unkes ne volt a rien mesfaire.*	never nor willed of anything misdeed.	never did he wish to do anything wrong.
181	*U que li reis deüst errer,*	Where which the king had to-go,	Where the king had to go,
182	*il n'out cure de desevrer;*	he not-had care of to-separate;	he did not care to separate from him;
183	*ensemble od lui tuz jurs alout,*	with among him all days he-went,	with him he always went,
184	*bien s'aparceit que il l'amout.*	well he-perceived that he him-loved.	and he perceived well that he loved him.
185	*Oëz aprés cument avint!*	Hear after what happened!	Hear what happened after!
186	*A une curt que li reis tint*	At a court which the king held	At a court which the king held
187	*tuz les baruns aveit mandez,*	all the barons he-had ordered,	he had ordered all the barons,
188	*cels ki furent de ses chasez,*	those which he-had of full fief,	those which he had fiefdom over,
189	*pur aidier sa feste a tenir*	for to-help his party to have	to contribute to his party

Marie de France - Bisclavret

	Old French	Literal	English
190	*e lui plus bel faire servir.*	and him more well made served.	and serve him more graciously.
191	*Li chevaliers i est alez,*	The knight he is gone,	The knight he has gone,
192	*richement e bien aturnez,*	richly and well dressed,	richly and well dressed,
193	*ki la femme Bisclavret ot.*	who had the-wife Bisclavret of.	who had the wife of Bisclavret.
194	*Il ne saveit ne ne quidot*	He not knew not no thought	He did not know and did not think
195	*qu'il le deüst trover si pres.*	which-that he would find so close.	that he would find him so close.
196	*Si tost cum il vint al palais*	As soon as he came to the-palace	As soon as he came to the palace
197	*e li Bisclavret l'aperceut,*	and him Bisclavret noticed,	and Bisclavret noticed him,
198	*de plein eslais vers lui curut:*	of full run towards him ran:	at full speed he ran towards him:
199	*as denz le prist, vers lui le trait.*	in teeth his seized, towards him he draws.	in his teeth he seized him, toward him he draws him.
200	*Ja li eüst mult grant laid fait,*	Now he would-have much great harm done,	Now he would have done great harm,
201	*ne fust li reis ki l'apela,*	not had the king him called,	If the king had not called him,
202	*d'une verge le manaça.*	with-a stick him threatened.	and threatened him with a stick.
203	*Dous feiz le volt mordre le jur.*	Two times he wanted to-bite him that-day.	Twice that day he wanted to bite him.
204	*Mult s'esmerveillent li plusur;*	Most astonished him more;	Most people were more astonished;
205	*kar unkes tel semblant ne fist*	because never had appeared not been-so	because he had never appeared like this
206	*vers nul hume que il veïst.*	toward any man whom he saw.	toward any man whom he saw.
207	*Ceo diënt tuit par la maisun*	Everyone said all by the house	Everyone in the house said
208	*qu'il nel fet mie senz raisun,*	that not act not-at-all without reason,	that he did not act without a reason,

Marie de France - Bisclavret

Old French	Literal	English
209 *mesfait li a, coment que seit,*	mistreatment he had, somehow which been,	some injury or mistreatment had somehow been done to him,
210 *kar volentiers se vengereit.*	because he-wanted to avenge-himself.	because he wanted to avenge himself.
211 *A cele feiz remest issi,*	At that-time nothing more happened,	At that time nothing more happened,
212 *tant que la feste departi;*	until that the party departed;	until the party had departed;
213 *e li barun unt pris cungié,*	and the barons they took leave,	and the barons took leave,
214 *a lur maisun sunt repairié.*	to their homes they went.	and went to their homes.
215 *Alez s'en est li chevaliers,*	Gone it is the knight,	Gone is the knight,
216 *mien esciënt tut as premiers,*	among it-seems all the first,	among the first it seems,
217 *que li Bisclavret asailli;*	which the Bisclavret assailed;	which the Bisclavret had attacked;
218 *n'est merveille s'il le haï.*	not-is wonder if-him he hated.	no wonder if he hated him.
219 *Ne fu puis guaires lungement,*	Not happened since much long-after,	It happened not long after this,
220 *(ceo m'est a vis, si cum j'entent),*	(such is as so, if with I-understand),	(such as it is, if I understand),
221 *qu'a la forest ala li reis,*	that to-the forest went the king,	that the king went to the forest,
222 *ki tant fu sages e curteis,*	who was so understanding and courteous,	who was so understanding and courteous,
223 *u li Bisclavret fu trovez;*	where the Bisclavret was found;	to where the Bisclavret was found;
224 *e il i est od lui alez.*	and he with was among him went.	and there with him he went.
225 *La nuit quant il s'en repaira,*	The night when he was returned,	In the night when he came back,
226 *en la cuntree herberja.*	in the country he-stayed.	in the country he stayed.
227 *La femme Bisclavret le sot.*	The woman Bisclavret the found-out.	The wife of Bisclavret found out.

Marie de France - Bisclavret

	Old French	Literal	English
228	*Avenantment s'apareillot.*	Attractively she-dressed.	Attractively she dressed.
229	*Al demain vait al rei parler,*	In the-morning went to-the king to-talk-with,	In the morning she went to see the king,
230	*riche present li fait porter.*	expensive present she does bring.	an expensive gift she brings him.
231	*Quant Bisclavret la veit venir,*	When Bisclavret her sees coming,	When Bisclavret sees her coming,
232	*nuls huem nel poeit retenir:*	none man not can retain-him:	no man can hold him back:
233	*vers li curut cum enragiez.*	towards her he-runs as-though enraged.	towards her he runs as though enraged.
234	*Oëz cum il s'est bien vengiez!*	Listen how he is well avenged!	Listen to how he is well avenged!
235	*Le nes li esracha del vis.*	Her nose he snatched from face.	Her nose he snatched from her face.
236	*Que li peüst il faire pis?*	What he worse he done could-have?	What worse could he have done?
237	*De tutes parz l'unt manacié;*	From all sides they threatened;	From all sides they threatened him;
238	*ja l'eüssent tut depescié,*	indeed they-would-have all dismembered,	indeed they would have dismembered him,
239	*quant uns sages huem dist al rei:*	when one wise man said to the-king:	when one wise man said to the king:
240	*Sire', fet il, entent a mei!*	'Sire', said he, 'listen to me!	Sire', he said, 'listen to me!'
241	*Ceste beste a esté od vus;*	This beast has been with you;	This beast has been with you;
242	*n'i a ore celui de nus*	none is presently that-one of us	none of us who are present
243	*ki ne l'ait veü lungement*	who not has known-him long	have not known him long
244	*e pres de lui alé sovent.*	and close of him gone often.	and been close with him often.
245	*Unkes mes hume ne tucha*	Never more man not harm	Never more did he harm any man
246	*ne felunie ne mustra,*	nor felony none commit,	Nor commit any felony,

Marie de France - Bisclavret

	Old French	Literal	English
247	*fors a la dame qu'ici vei.*	except to the woman who-here you-see.	except in the case of the woman you see here.
248	*Par cele fei que jeo vus dei,*	By that faith that I you owe,	By that faith I owe you,
249	*alkun curuz a il vers li*	some anger has he against her	he has some anger against her
250	*e vers sun seignur altresi.*	and against her husband also.	and against her husband also.
251	*Ceo est la femme al chevalier*	This is the wife of the-knight	This is the wife of the knight
252	*que tant suliëz aveir chier,*	whom that previously have loved,	whom you used to love,
253	*ki lung tens a esté perduz,*	who long held that was lost,	who for such a long time was lost,
254	*ne seümes qu'est devenuz.*	nor knew what became-of.	nor known what had become of him.
255	*Kar metez la dame en destreit,*	Therefore place the woman with difficulty,	Therefore force that woman's hand,
256	*s'alcune chose vus direit,*	if-some thing you tells,	so that she might tell you something,
257	*pur quei ceste beste la het.*	for what this beast her hates.	why this beast hates her.
258	*Faites li dire s'el le set!*	Makes her say if-she this knows!	Make her say if she knows why!
259	*Meinte merveille avum veüe*	Many wonders have-we seen	Many wonders we have seen
260	*ki en Bretaigne est avenue'.*	which in Brittany that happened.	which in Brittany that happened.
261	*Li reis a sun cunseil creü.*	The king of his counsel believed.	The king believed his counsel.
262	*Le chevalier a retenu;*	The knight was retained;	The knight was retained;
263	*de l'altre part la dame a prise*	of the-other part the woman was taken-aside	on the other hand, the woman was taken aside
264	*e en mult grant destresce mise.*	and then much great distress questioned.	and then distressed with many questions.
265	*Tant par destresce e par poür*	As-much by distress and by fear	As much by distress and by fear

Marie de France - Bisclavret

	Old French	Literal	English
266	tut li cunta de sun seignur,	all she recounted of her husband,	she recounted all of her husband,
267	coment ele l'aveit traï	how she had betrayed	how she had betrayed him
268	e sa despueille li toli,	and how clothes his taken-away,	and how his clothes had been taken away,
269	l'aventure qu'il li cunta,	the-adventure which-of she recounted,	she told him of the adventure,
270	e que devint e u ala;	and what became and where he-went;	and what became of him and where he went;
271	puis que ses dras li ot toluz,	after that his clothes she away took,	after she took his clothes away,
272	ne fu en sun païs veüz;	not was he in country seen;	he was no longer seen in the country;
273	tresbien quidot e bien creeit	very-well thought that well believed	she thought and very well believed
274	que la beste Bisclavret seit.	that the beast Bisclavret to-be.	that the beast was Bisclavret.
275	Li reis demande sa despueille.	The king asked for the-clothing.	The king asks for the clothing.
276	U bel li seit u pas nel vueille,	Whether well he to-be or not nor want,	Whether he wants it or not,
277	ariere la fet aporter,	to-him it had brought,	to him it was brought,
278	al Bisclavret la fist doner.	to Bisclavret the has-it given.	to Bisclavret has it given.
279	Quant il l'orent devant lui mise,	When they had before him set,	When they put it before him,
280	ne s'en prist guarde en nule guise.	not did-he pay attention in no way.	he did not pay attention in any way.
281	Li prozdum le rei apela,	The worthy-man who the-king addressed,	The worthy man who addressed the king,
282	cil ki primes le cunseilla.	he who first him counselled.	he who first advised him.
283	Sire, ne faites mie bien!	'Sire, not done not-at-all well!	Sire, it is not done well at all!'
284	Cist nel fereit pur nule rien,	The-last among doing by any nothing,	The last thing he will do,
285	que devant vus ses dras reveste	that before your sight clothes re-dress	is re-dress before your sight
286	ne mut la semblance de beste.	nor change his appearance from the-beast.	nor change his appearance from the beast.

Marie de France - Bisclavret

	Old French	Literal	English
287	Ne savez mie que ceo munte.	You know not that this very-important.	You do not know that this is very important.
288	Mult durement en a grant hunte.	Very hard is a great shame.	Very hard is the great shame.
289	En tes chambres le fai mener	In your rooms him let be-taken	Let him be taken to your rooms,
290	e la despueille od lui porter;	and there clothes with him brought;	And have clothes brought to him;
291	une grant piece l'i laissuns.	a great part him let-us-leave.	And let us leave him for a time.
292	S'il devient huem, bien le verruns'.	if-he becomes a-man, well this we-will-see.	Whether he becomes a man, we will see.
293	Li reis meïsmes l'en mena	The king himself he there took	The king himself took him there
294	e tuz les hus sur lui ferma.	and all the doors behind him closed.	and all the doors behind him closed.
295	Al chief de piece i est alez;	At the-end of the-time there he went;	At the end of a time he went there;
296	dous baruns a od lui menez.	two barons that with him took.	he took two barons with him.
297	En la chambre entrerent tuit trei.	Unto the room entered all three.	All three entered the room.
298	Sur le demeine lit al rei	On his own bed the king's	On the king's own bed
299	truevent dormant le chevalier.	they-find sleeping the knight.	they find the knight sleeping.
300	Li reis le curut enbracier;	The king him ran to-embrace;	The king ran to embrace him;
301	plus de cent feiz l'acole e baise.	more than a-hundred times embraces and kisses.	more than a hundred times, he embraces and kisses him.
302	Si tost cum il pot aveir aise,	As soon as he could have facility,	As soon as he had the opportunity,
303	Tute sa terre li rendi,	All his land to-him returned,	He returned all his land to him,
304	plus li duna que jeo ne di.	more him gave than I can tell.	and gave him more than I can tell.
305	La femme a del païs ostee	The woman of from the-country banned	The woman was banned from the country

Marie de France - Bisclavret

	Old French	Literal	English
306	e chaciee de la cuntree.	and chased out-of the country.	and chased out of the country.
307	Cil s'en ala ensemble od li,	The-one who along together with her,	The one who went with her,
308	pur qui sun seignur ot traï.	for whom her husband had betrayed.	for whom she had betrayed her husband.
309	Enfanz en a asez eüz,	Children with of many they-had,	They had many children,
310	puis unt esté bien cuneüz	could they be well known	they were well known
311	e del semblant e del visage:	by of appearance and of face:	by their appearance and by their faces:
312	plusurs des femmes del lignage,	many of women of lineage,	many women of their lineage,
313	c'est veritez, senz nes sunt nees	it-is true, without noses they-were born	it is true, were born with out noses
314	e si viveient esnasees.	and thus they-live noselessly.	and so they lived noselessly.
315	L'aventure qu'avez oïe	The-story which you-heard	The story which you heard
316	veraie fu, n'en dutez mie.	true was, do-not doubt not-at-all.	was true, do not doubt at all.
317	De Bisclavret fu fez li lais	Of Bisclavret was composed this lay	This lay was composed of Bisclavret
318	pur remembrance a tuz dis mais.	for remembrance of all tell more.	for remembrance of all more to tell.

Word List *(Old French to English)*

Old French	English

A, a

Old French	English
a	a, against, and, as, at, had, has, he, in, is, of, on, that, then, to, under, up to, was
abatre	destroy, knock down
abevrez	drink
acreanter	agree, allow, promise
ad	against, in, on, to, up to
adenz	face downwards
adober	arm oneself
adurer	worship
afaire	matter
ai	have
aidier	to-help
aiglantier	wild rose
aiglent	wild rose
ainc	earlier, rather
ains	earlier, rather
ainz	earlier, rather
aire	appearance
aise	facility
aistre	be
Al	at, in, of, the, to, to-the
ala	along, he-went, of, of-the, went
alaine	blast, breath
alé	gone
aleine	blast, breath
aler	go
alez	go, gone, went
alkun	some
alme	somebody, soul
alne	ell
alout	he-went, went
alt	high, important, strong
altain	deep, high
altre	other
altresi	also
Alum	let-us
amant	lover
ame	somebody, soul
amé	loved
amee	loved
amer	love
amez	a-love, loved
ami	friend
amie	friend
amis	friend
amistié	friendship
amor	love
amot	loved
an	year
anel	ring
angregier	become more painful, grow worse
anima	soul
anme	somebody, soul
anor	esteem, fief, honor, respect
anpur	for the sake of
aparant	visible
aparceüz	aware
apela	addressed, he-called
apeler	accuse, call, summon
apercevoir	know, notice
apert	manifest, open, visible
aporter	brought
apres	after, afterwards
aprés	after
ardoir	burn
ardre	burn
argent	money, riches, silver
ariere	back, to-him
arire	back
ariver	arrive
arme	somebody, soul
arrere	back
arriere	back
art	craft, liberal art
as	in, the
asailli	assailed
aseüré	assured
asez	many, much, very well

21

Word List (Old French to English)

Old French	English	*Old French*	English
asproier	prosecute, torment	*baisier*	kiss
assanler	assemble, call together, meet	*balt*	full of fervor, happy
		barbe	beard
assembler	assemble, call together, meet	*baron*	brave knight, brave warrior
asseoir	lay siege, place, set up	*barun*	barons
assés	many, much, very well	*baruns*	barons
astenir	keep from	*bataille*	battle
ataindre	catch, reach, regain	*Beals*	handsome
atorner	prepare, turn	*bealz*	gentle
atot	with	*bec*	beak
aturnez	dressed	*bel*	beautiful, beloved, dear, handsome, well
aucun	some		
aussi	also, likewise	*ben*	good, good fortune, well-being
aut	high, important, strong		
avant	forward	*ber*	baron
avec	with	*beste*	beast, the-beast
aveir	be, have	*bevre*	drink
aveit	had, he-had	*bien*	good, good fortune, many, much, really, well, well-being
avenant	attractive, beautiful		
Avenantment	attractively		
avenement	arrival	*Bisclavret*	werewolf
avenir	arrive, frequently, happen	*blanc*	white
		blandi	cajoled
avenue	happened	*bois*	forest, tree
aviler	abandon, disgrace	*bon*	good
avint	happened	*bonement*	very-well
aviser	appreciate, look at, recognize, see	*bons*	good
		bos	forest, tree
avoc	with	*boscages*	woods
avoir	be, have	*bouche*	mouth
avreie	could	*braire*	shout, sing
avrez	have	*Bretaigne*	Brittany
avuec	with	*Bretan*	Breton
avum	have-we	*buche*	mouth
		buissun	bush

B, b

C, c

bacheler	page, young knight aspirant, young man	*cadable*	catapult
		car	because, for
bachelor	page, young knight aspirant, young man	*cas*	affair, event, fall
		castel	castle
baillier	give, own, receive	*cavee*	dug-out
bailliz	treated	*ce*	it, that, this
baisa	kissed		
baise	kisses		

Word List (Old French to English)

Old French	English
ceanz	in here
cel	the
cela	concealed
cele	such, that, that-time, this
celer	conceal
cels	those
celui	for-him, that-one, who-him
cent	a-hundred
ceo	behold-this, everyone, it, such, that, this
cervel	brains
Cest	this
c'est	it-is
ceste	this
ceu	it, that, this
cez	these
chacerai	will-hunt
chaciee	chased
chacier	hunt
Chaciez	chase
chaeir	fall
chaitif	miserable
chaloir	concern, matter
chambre	chamber, room, royal apartment, territory
chambres	rooms
chant	melody, song
chanter	sing
chapele	chapel
char	flesh, meat
charn	flesh, meat
chartre	agreement, letter
chasez	fief
chasser	hunt
chastel	castle
chemin	path
cheoir	fall
cher	beloved, expensive
chevalier	knight, the-knight
chevaliers	gentleman, knight, knights
chevauchie	expedition, ride
chief	head, the-end
chien	dogs
chiens	dogs
chier	love, loved
chierté	fondness
choisi	saw
chose	affair, creature, thing
chrestien	christian
ci	here
ciel	heaven
cil	he, him, that, the-one, they, this-he
Cist	the-last, this
cit	city, town
citet	city, town
clameor	appeal
clamer	call, confess, proclaim
clementiam	grace
clerc	clerk
clerge	clerk
coer	heart
cointe	clever, elegant, refined
colomb	dove, pigeon
colon	dove, pigeon
colpe	mistake, sin
com	as, in order that, when
comandé	commanded
comander	give, order, recommend
comencier	begin, start
coment	how, somehow
comme	as, when
compaigne	troops
comunalment	together
concreidre	give in
congié	leave, permission, permission to leave
conquerre	capture, conquer
conseilleor	advisor, counsellor
conseillier	advisor, counsellor
conserrer	deprive, resign
consirrer	deprive, resign
consolation	consolation
conte	count
contenant	appearance, demeanour, expression
conter	count, relate
contre	against, compared with
contredire	oppose, resist

Word List (Old French to English)

Old French	English	*Old French*	English
converse	about	*curteis*	courteous
conversez	about	*cururent*	chased
convoier	escort	*curut*	anger, he-runs, ran, running
cope	mistake, sin		
cor	heart, horn	*curuz*	anger
corn	horn		
corocier	afflict, anger		
corpe	mistake, sin		
corre	run		
cors	body, heart		
cose	affair, creature, thing		
couchier	lie down		
creanter	agree, grant		
creeit	believed		
creistre	grow		
creü	believed		
crie	asks-for		
criem	fear		
crier	shout		
croistre	grow		
cruese	hollow		
cuer	heart, my-heart		
cuidier	think		
cuire	burn, cook		
culchier	slept		
cum	as, as-though, how, in order that, with		
cument	what		
cumfaitement	in-such-way		
cumpaignuns	companions		
cuneüz	known		
cunfort	comfort		
cungié	leave		
cunquerre	capture, conquer		
cunseil	counsel		
cunseilla	counselled		
cunta	recounted		
cunté	recounted		
cunteneit	led-himself		
cunter	to-recount		
cuntredit	opposition		
cuntree	country		
curage	heart		
cure	anxiety, care		
curios	careful		
curt	court		

D, d

Old French	English
daignier	deign
dales	along, next to
dallĂŠ	along, next to
dalles	along, next to
dam	lord, sir
damage	harm, trouble
dame	dame, lady, madam, woman
damoiselle	girl of noble birth
dan	lord, sir
de	by, from, of, out-of, than, to, with
de vers	from the direction of, in the direction of
deable	devil
debonaire	noble, sweet
deciré	tear
deçoivre	deceive, mislead
dedenz	inside
deduire	lead, live
degré	staircase
dei	finger, owe
del	from, of, of-this, to
delé	next to; beside
deleiz	next to; beside
deles	next to; beside
delicios	delicious
d'els	be
demain	the-morning
demanda	questions
demandasse	to-ask
demande	asked
demandé	asked
demander	ask, ask for
demandez	ask, sought-for
demeine	own
demoree	delay, stay

Word List (Old French to English)

Old French	English	*Old French*	English
demorer	remain, stay	dol	grief, suffering
demostrer	explaine, indicate, show	dolent	sorrowful, wetched
denz	teeth	dolor	pain, suffering
departi	departed	dolur	pain
depescié	dismembered	dolz	gentle, sweet
des	of, of-them	donc	then, therefore
descendre	descend, dismount	doner	give, given
desconfire	defeat, demolish	dont	of which, of whom, whose
descovri	revealed	dormant	sleeping
descuplé	released	doter	be afraid, doubt
desevrer	to-separate	dous	gentle, sweet, two
desi	until	dras	clothes
desos	under	dreit	straight
desous	under	droit	direct, proper, right
despueille	clothes, the-clothing	drue	mistress
destreit	difficulty	duc	duke
destresce	distress	duel	grief, suffering
deu	god, god's	dulz	sweet
deüst	had, would	d'ume	of-a-man
devant	before, in front of, in the presence of	duna	gave
deveneit	became	dunc	so
devenir	become	d'une	of-one, with-a
devenuz	became-of	duné	dedicated
devers	from the direction of, in the direction of	dunt	of which, of whom, which, whose
devez	should	dur	cruel, hard, unrefined
deviene	become	durement	greatly, hard, sorely, very
devient	becomes	durrai	grant
devindrent	became	duter	doubt
devint	became	dutez	doubt
devoir	have to		
devorer	devour		
devure	devours		
di	day, tell		
diavle	devil		
die	you		
diënt	said		
dirai	will-tell		
dire	say, tell		
direit	tells		
dis	tell		
dist	said, tell		
dites	tell		
divers	various		
doi	finger		

E, e

Old French	English
e	and, by, of, that
ed	and
eim	love
eissil	ruin, wretchedness
el	he, in, she
Ele	he, she
element	energy, force, god
emparenté	of noble lineage
empedement	persecution
empeindre	blow, protrude

Word List (Old French to English)

Old French	English	*Old French*	English
empereor	emperor	entent	listen
en	and, go, he, in, into, is, of it, on, on top of, then, to, unto, with	entente	reason
		entier	entire
		entiers	entire
enbracier	to-embrace	entre	among, between, in the midst of
encombrer	overload		
encontre	against, to, towards	entrepris	unhappy person
encontrer	meet	entrerent	entered
encor	still, yet	enui	pain, torment
encore	still, yet	envers	towards
encuntré	encountered	erbre	grass
end	subsequently	errer	to-go
endreit	immediately, precisely, right, ways	ert	was
		es	in-those
enemi	devil, enemy	esbai	frightened, surprised, troubled
Enfanz	children		
enferm	crippled, ill, unhealthy, weak	esbanir	amuse
		eschec	booty, loot
enfermeté	illness, physical or moral weakness	eschecs	chess
		esciënt	it-seems
enfern	hell	escïent	knowledge
engagier	commit	escolter	listen to, pay attention to
engeignier	deceive, invent, seduce		
engeindre	cause	escremir	fence
engendrer	cause	escrier	cry out, shout
engien	cheating, skill	escrimer	fence
engignier	deceive, invent, seduce	escu	shield
engin	cheating, skill	esfrei	fear
enne	not	esguardez	look-at
ennui	grief	eslais	assault
enoi	pain, torment	esleecier	rejoice
enor	esteem, fief, honor, respect	esmaier	be dismayed
		esnasees	noselessly
enorter	exhort, seduce, urge	espee	sword
enpur	for the sake of	espés	thick
enquis	inquired, queried	Espleitiez	hurry
enragié	furious	esposer	marry
enragiez	enraged	espuse	wife
enseigna	indicated	espusee	married
enseigne	war cry	esracha	snatched
enseignier	inform, point out, teach	essil	ruin, wretchedness
ensemble	together, with	est	are, he, is, that, was
ensemble od	together with	estait	standing
ent	subsequently	esté	be, been, was
entendre	hear, pay attention, try, understand	esteit	he-was, noble, stayed, was-he
entendu	heard		

Word List (Old French to English)

Old French	English
ester	be, remain, stand, was
estes	are
estor	battle, noise, tumult
estorm	battle, noise, tumult
estre	be, condition, life, way of life
estrié	stirrup
estude	study, zeal
estudie	study, zeal
estut	stand
et	and
euc	this
eure	hour, time
eüsse	were
eüst	would-have
eüz	they-had

F, f

Old French	English
fai	let
faim	desire, hunger
faire	do, done, made, make
faiseit	made
fait	does, done, has-done, said
faites	done, make, makes
faldestoed	folding chair for important person, throne
faldestuef	folding chair for important person, throne
faldestuel	folding chair for important person, throne
fals	false
faus	false
favele	lie, story
fei	faith, honor
feindre	do nothing, shy away
feintise	deceit, pretense
feiz	nothing, put, time, times
felunie	felony
femme	the-wife, wife, woman
femmes	women
fenir	end, stop
fer	iron, weapon
fereit	doing
ferez	will-do
ferma	closed
feruz	beaten
feste	party
fet	act, had, said
feu	family, fire
fez	composed
fiance	promise
fier	fierce, proud, strong
fiere	hit
figure	character, form, person
fil	son
filer	spin
fille	daughter
filuel	godson, son
finir	end, stop
fist	been-so, has-it
flor	flower
florir	flower
foi	faith, honor
fol	crazy
foler	harm
forest	forest
forez	forests
forfait	committed
forment	greatly, very, very much
fors	except, out, outside
fort	fierce, hard, strong
fou	family, fire
fraindre	break
frans	engaging
freindre	break
frere	brother
fromage	cheese
fu	became, happened, is, so, was
fuier	abandon, flee from
fuir	abandon, flee from
furent	he-had, were
fusse	had-been
fussent	would-be
fust	had, was

Word List (Old French to English)

Old French	English	*Old French*	English
		halberc	hauberk
		halt	high, important, strong
G, g		hardi	bold, brave
		hastif	swift
gab	jest	have	dark, sick, somber
gant	glove	herbergier	lodge, receive as guest, shelter
garant	defense, protection		
garder	guard, watch over	herberja	he-stayed
garent	defense, protection	het	hates
garnement	decorative object	home	man
Garulf	Garulf	honestét	honor
gent	beautiful, fair, handsome, people, race	honore	honored
		honte	disgrace, shame
gentil	brave, noble	hors	except, out, out of
gesir	lie	huem	a-man, man
geter	reject, throw, utter	hui	this-day
gisir	to-lie	huit	eight
giter	reject, throw, utter	huitaves	octave
gloire	glory	hum	he, him
grabatum	simple bed	hume	man
grant	great, large, tall	humes	men
granter	agree, grant	hunte	shame
granz	grand	hus	doors
gré	Greek		
gri	Greek	**I, i**	
grieu	Greek		
griu	Greek		
guaires	much	i	he, i, is, there, with
gualdine	forest	Iceste	this
guarde	attention	ici	here
guardent	guard	iestre	be
guarderent	guarded	Il	he, it, they
guardez	take-care	ilec	there
guarie	relieved	ille	island
guerpir	abandon, abandoning, leave	iluec	there
		iluoc	there
guerre	trouble, war	ire	anger, distress
guerredoner	reward	iré	angry, distressed, furious
guise	manner, way		
gunfanuner	standard bearer	irié	angry, distressed, furious
		isle	island
H, h		issi	happened, here, so, thus
ha	ha, hello	issil	ruin, wretchedness
haï	hated	issir	come out, go out
haine	hatred		

28

Word List (Old French to English)

Old French	English

J, j

Old French	English
ja	already, at once, ever, indeed, never, now
Jadis	days-passed
jai	already, at once, now
jambe	leg
j'entent	i-understand
jeo	I
jes	I
jeu	I
jo	I, me
joer	play
joi	joy
joie	joy
joieus	full of joy
joius	joyous
jol	I
jor	day
jorn	day
jornee	day's journey
jou	I
jur	that-day
jurs	days
jusqu'a	as far as, up to

K, k

Old French	English
kar	because, come, therefore
ki	him, of, that, which, who

L, l

Old French	English
la	had, her, his, is, it, of, that, the, there, to-the
l'a	that, this
l'acola	he-embraced
l'acole	embraces
l'ai	of-him
laid	harm
lais	lay, lays
laissier	abandon, leave, left, let
laissuns	let-us-leave
l'ait	has
l'altre	the-other
l'amout	him-loved
l'anguissa	anguish
l'apela	called
l'apelent	they-call
l'aperceut	noticed
l'aveit	had, her-had, him-had
l'aventure	the-adventure, the-event, the-story
le	he, her, him, his, it, one, the, this, who
leal	legitimate, loyal
lee	wide
legier	light, light-hearted, supple
l'en	her, him, there
l'enveia	she-sent-for
les	his, let, the
leur	their
l'eüssent	they-would-have
lever	lift up
lez	near
li	he, her, him, his, she, the, this, to-him, was
l'i	him
lié	happy, joyful
lier	bind
liet	happy, joyful
liez	happy
ligier	light, light-hearted, supple
lignage	family, lineage
lil	lily
lit	bed
liue	mile
live	mile
livre	book, inventory
loër	praise
l'oï	that-heard
loial	legitimate, loyal
loier	bind
loigier	light, light-hearted, supple
loin	far, far away
loing	far, far away, long

Word List (Old French to English)

Old French	English	*Old French*	English
lonc	far, far away, long	*manjuer*	eat
long	far, long	*mar*	in vain, wrongly
longement	for a long time, long	*masse*	mass
lor	their	*mat*	exhausted, feeble, sad
l'orent	had	*me*	I, me, to-me
losenja	praised	*mectre*	put
l'ot	before	*mei*	from-me, me, mine, to-me
l'ourent	caught	*meine*	takes
lui	he, him	*meins*	fewer, less
luin	far, far away	*meinte*	many
lung	long	*meïsmes*	himself, myself
lungement	long, long-after	*mels*	better, rather
l'unt	they	*m'en*	to-me
lur	let, their	*mena*	took
		menace	menace
		mener	be-taken, lead, show, take

M, m

Old French	English	*Old French*	English
ma	my	*menestier*	profession, service
magne	great	*menez*	took
maindre	remain, stay	*mentir*	betray, deny, fail, lie
mains	fewer, less	*m'entremet*	i-begin
maint	many, many a	*menu*	quickly
maintenant	immediately, soon	*menut*	quickly
mais	but, further, more, rather	*mer*	pure, sea
maisnie	army, household	*merci*	grace, mercy, pity
maisniee	army, household	*mercie*	thanks
maison	house	*mere*	mother
maisun	home, homes, house	*merveille*	marvel, marvellously, what is surprising, wonder, wonders
mal	bad, badly, disaster, evil, harm, illness, mean, wretched	*mes*	but, furthermore, he, me, more, my, with
malement	badly	*mescroire*	refuse to believe, suspect
malfé	demon, devil	*meserrez*	misguided
Mals	bad	*mesfacent*	harm
maltalent	anger	*mesfaire*	misdeed
m'amur	my-love	*mesfait*	mistreatment
manaça	threatened	*mesprendre*	commit a crime, make a mistake
manace	menace	*message*	message, messenger
manacié	threatened	*m'est*	is
manda	sent-for	*met*	go, put, puts
mandez	ordered	*metez*	place
maneit	lived	*metre*	put
mangier	eat	*mettre*	put
maniere	intention, way		

Word List (Old French to English)

Old French	English
mie	not, not-at-all
miels	better, rather
mien	among
mier	pure
millier	thousand
miracle	miracle
mis	treated
mise	questioned, set
moine	monk
moins	fewer, less
molt	many, much, very
mon	my
monie	monk
mont	mountain
montaigne	mountain
moralité	character, lesson
mordre	to-bite
morir	die, kill
mort	death
mot	word
mout	many, much, very
mult	many, most, much, very
mun	my, to-me
mund	world
munte	very-important
mur	wall
mustra	commit
mut	change

N, n

Old French	English
n'a	not-has
nate	matting
ne	and not, can, he, naught, no, no-longer, none, nor, not, you
nees	born
nef	ship
nel	among, nor, not
nen	do-not, not
n'en	about, do-not, nor, not
nes	nose, noses
n'est	not-is
neveu	grandson, nephew
nevot	grandson, nephew
ni	and not, nor
n'i	never-will, none, No-one
nïent	nothing
nïent	not at all
noblement	nobly
nom	name, title
nomer	call, name
non	name, not, title
noncier	announce, tell
nonque	never
nonsavoir	ignorance
Norman	Normans
nos	we
nostre	our
n'ot	before
n'out	not-had
nuit	night
nul	any, anyone, no, not any
nule	any, no, not
nuls	none
nun	the-name
nus	us, we
nuz	nude

O, o

Old French	English
o	or, this, with
ocire	kill
od	among, with
odir	hear
oeuil	eye
Oëz	hear, listen
of	with
oi	today
oï	heard, i-hear
oïe	you-heard
oil	eye
oir	hear
oïr	hear
oisel	bird
olifant	ivory horn
om	one
ome	man

Word List (Old French to English)

Old French	English
on	one
onor	esteem, fief, honor, respect
onques	ever, once
or	gold, just, now
oraison	prayer, speech
ore	hour, now, presently, time
orer	pray
orison	prayer, speech
osasse	dare
osberc	hauberk
oser	dare
ostee	banned
ostel	dwelling, house
ot	away, had, of, with
otrei	grant
otrier	agree, grant
otroier	agree, grant
ou	this, where

P, p

Old French	English
pagien	heathen, pagan
paien	heathen, pagan
paile	precious cloth
pain	bread
paine	suffering, torment
païs	country, the-country
paistre	feed
palais	the-palace
pance	belly, stomach
paor	fear
Par	by, by reason of, through
par mi	in the middle, through
parage	family, origin, rank
parament	finery, precious object
pardon	grace, permission
pardoner	forgive, pardon
parent	father, parent
parlement	conversation, meeting, word
parler	speak, talk, to-talk-with
parmi	in the middle, through

Old French	English
parole	speech, word
part	part, portion
partez	part
partir	part-with, to-part
partirai	will-part
parvenir	arrive
parz	sides
pas	not
pau	few, little
pechié	mistake, sin
pecier	smash to pieces
peine	suffering, torment
pendre	hang
pener	suffer, torture
penser	pay attention, think
peor	fear
perdeit	lost, missed
perdrai	destroy
perdre	lose, loss, perish
perduz	lost, to-lose
pere	father
peril	danger
perir	destroy, perish
perte	destruction, fall
pes	peace
pestre	feed
petit	little, small
peüst	could, worse
peüz	food
pié	feet, foot
piece	part, piece, segment, the-time
piere	prison, stone
pierre	prison, stone
pin	pine tree
pis?	could-have
plain	full
plaindre	complain, mourn, regret
plaire	please
plein	full
ploier	bend, yield
plorer	cry, shed tears
pluisor	several
plus	more, most
plusor	several
plusur	many, more

32

Word List (Old French to English)

Old French	English
plusurs	many
poeir	be able, can
poeit	can, could
poi	but, few, little
poier	be able, can
polle	girl
pooir	be able, can
por	for
porchacier	pursue, seek
porent	could-they
porofrir	present
port	harbour, port
porter	bring, brought, carry, wear
porveor	purveyor
post	after
pot	could
pou	few, little
poür	fear, horror
pout	could
poverté	misery, poverty
povre	poor
preie	plunder
preiee	courted
preier	beg, beseech, pray
premiers	first
prendre	seize, take, take hold of
prent	receives
pres	close
pres de	close to
present	present
presenter	bring before the judge, offer, present
prester	lend
priement	prayer
prier	beg, beseech, pray
primes	first
pris	prize, seized, took
prise	taken-aside
prisier	appreciate, esteem
prison	captivity, prison
prist	pay, seized
privez	close
proisier	appreciate, esteem
prozdum	worthy-man
pucele	girl, maiden, servant
pui	hill, mountain
puis	after, could, since, subsequently, then
pur	all, because, by, for, therefore
purpensa	purposed

Q, q

Old French	English
qu'a	that
Qu'ai	what-have
quanque	all that
Quant	when
quar	because, for
qu'avez	which
que	for, than, that, what, when, which, who
quei	what
quel	what, which
qu'el	with
queloigne	distaff
qu'en	that-in
quenoille	distaff
quere	ask, look for, want
querre	ask, asking-for, look for, want
querrez	ask
qu'est	what
qui	that, what, who
qu'ici	who-here
quidot	thought
quidouent	thought-they
qu'il	that, what, which, which-of, which-that
quinze	fifteen
quis	he
qu'um	of-him

R, r

Old French	English
rage	rage
raine	queen
raison	reason, speech, word
raisun	reason
ravine	theft

Word List (Old French to English)

Old French	English	*Old French*	English
ravoir	have back	riche	expensive, generous, powerful, strong
ré	stake		
reclamer	beg, call upon, invoke	richement	richly
reconoistre	recognize	rien	any, anything, creature, nothing, person, thing
recreant	cowardly, exhausted		
redoter	be afraid, fear	rien?	nothing
redut	dread	roi	king
refaire	repair	roine	queen
regal	of the king, royal	rompre	break, burst
regem	king	rose	rose
regne	country, kingdom	rover	ask, call upon, order
rei	king, king's, stake, the-king	rue	street, village
reine	queen		
reis	king		
relef	remains, scraps		

S, s

Old French	English
sa	for, his, how, this
sages	understanding, wise
sai	i-know
saige	clever, educated
saint	holy
sairement	oath
saive	clever, educated
s'alcune	if-some
s'alout	next-to
saluer	greet, salute
salvage	savage
s'amur	for-the-love-of, love
sanc	blood
sanglent	bloody
santé	health, well-being
s'aparceit	he-perceived
s'apareillot	she-dressed
saveit	knew, knowing
s'aventure	his-adventure
savez	know
savoir	know
se	he, if, of, she, to
se coucher	lie down
se dementer	lament
se departir	go away, leave
se faire	be
se hasteier	hasten
se haster	hasten
se pasmer	faint, swoon
se reposer	rest

Old French	English
remanoir	remain, resist, stay
remembrance	rememberance
remest	more, remained
ren	creature, person, thing
rendi	returned
rendre	give, return
rendu	returned
renier	abjure, deny
renoier	abjure, deny
repaira	returned
repairié	went
repairiez	returned
requerre	ask, beseech
requise	desired
resort	defense, remedy, restriction
resovenir	remember
respit	delay
respondre	answer
respunt	responded
retenir	retain-him
retenu	retained
retor	return
retorn	return
reveler	make known, reveal, revolt
reveste	re-dress
revienc	return
rez	stake

Word List (Old French to English)

Old French	English	Old French	English
seans	in here	siwant	followed
secle	earthly life, world	soens	his
secorer	go to the help of	sol	alone
seiez	be	soloir	be accustomed
seignor	lord	som	sleep
seignur	husband, lord, sires	some	sleep
seit	been, to-be	son	his
s'el	if-she	soner	sound, utter
semblance	appearance	sor	above, on, over, to
semblant	appearance, appeared	sos	under
semblereit	would-look-like	sostenir	support, sustain
semeine	week	sot	found-out
sempre	always, immediately	soure	above, on, over, to
sempres	always, immediately	sout	knew
sen	direction, sense	sovent	frequently, many, often, time-to-time
s'en	did-he, if, it, then, was, who	soz	under
sens	direction, sense	sucurs	help
sentier	path	suens	people
sentir	feel, smell	sui	am, i-am
senz	without	suleit	used
seoir	be seated, sit	suliëz	previously
sereie	I-would-be	s'umilie	is-humbled
serre	prison	sun	a, her, his, in
servant	servant	suner	sound, utter
servir	serve, served	sunt	are, they, they-were
servise	devotion, favor, service, task	sur	above, behind, on, over, sure, to
ses	full, his, sight	sus	above, up
s'esfrea	she-was-terrified	Suventes	repeatedly
s'esmerveillent	astonished	suz	above, under, up
s'est	is	suzprist	under-pressed
set	knows, seven		
seü	known		
seule	earthly life, world		
seümes	knew		

T, t

Old French	English
seur	above, on, over, sure, to		
si	and, and moreover, and thus, as, but, if, so, that much, that way, thus, yet	table	game, table
		tans	time, weather
		tant	as, as-much, so, so much, so-much, such, such-time, that, until
s'i	thus	tantost	immediately
siecle	earthly life, world	tel	had, has, much, such
S'il	if-he, if-him, whether	temple	forehead, temple
sire	husband, my-lord, sire	tendrement	tenderly
sis	her		

Word List (Old French to English)

Old French	English	*Old French*	English
tenir	consider, have, hold, keep, seize	*trovez*	found
tens	held, time, weather	*truevent*	they-find
tenu	beheld	*trusqu'*	until, up to
terme	period, period of time, term	*tu*	you
		tucha	harm
termine	period of time	*tuit*	all
terre	country, earth, land	*turnez*	returned
tes	your	*tut*	all
teste	head	*tute*	all
tindrent	had	*tutejur*	all-the-day
tint	held, travelled, travels	*tutes*	all
tirer	pull	*tuz*	all, totally
toli	taken-away		
tolir	cut off, take off		
toluz	took		

U, u

Old French	English
ton	your
tor	tower
torner	return, turn
tornoier	tourney, whirl around
tort	mistake
tost	immediately, quickly, soon
tot	all, completely, entirely, every, whole
traï	betrayed
trair	betray
traist	drew-close
trait	draws
traïz	betrayed
travailliez	striving
trei	three
treis	three

Old French	English
u	or, where, whether
ubliër	forget
ue	today
ui	today
un	a, one
unc	never
uncore	still, yet
une	a, an, one
unkes	never
uns	one
unt	then, they

V, v

Old French	English
trembler	tremble
trenchier	cut
trente et quatre	thirty four
tres	much, very
tresbien	very-well
trespasser	cross, go by, pass
tresprendre	overcome completely
tresqu'	until, up to
tristece	horror, sadness
trois	three
trop	excessively, extremely, too much
trover	find

Old French	English
vaillant	valiant
vain	empty, weak
vait	goes, went
veer	forbid, refuse
vei	you-see
veie	road, way
veil	old
veintre	conquer, overcome, vanquish
veisins	neighbours
veïst	saw
veit	sees
veiz	time
vendra	comes
veneür	hunters

Word List (Old French to English)

Old French	English	*Old French*	English
venez	come	voz	your
vengereit	avenge-himself	vueil	i-want, i-wish, want
vengiez	avenged	vueille	want
venir	come, coming, go	vuide	empty
venue	arrival	vuit	empty
veoir	see	vus	answer, i-wish, you, you-have, your, yours
verai	real, true		
veraie	true		
verge	stick		
vergier	garden, orchard		
veritez	true		
vermeille	crimson		
verruns	we-will-see		
vers	against, to, toward, towards, went		
vert	green		
vertu	might, power, strength		
vestuz	dressed		
vet	goes, there		
veü	known-him, seen		
vieil	old		
viez	old		
vif	live		
vilain	bad, ugly		
vin	wine		
vint	came		
virge	virgin		
virginitét	christian purity, spiritual purity		
vis	face, so		
visage	face		
viseter	observe, visit		
vit	saw		
viveient	they-live		
voir	indeed, true, truly		
voirement	really		
vois	go, noise, voice, word		
voiz	noise, voice, word		
voleit	wanted		
volentiers	gladly, he-wanted, willing		
voler	fly		
voloir	want		
volt	wanted, wants, willed		
vos	you		
vostre	your		

Word List *(English to Old French)*

English	Old French	English	Old French
		and moreover	*si*
		and not	*ne, ni*
		and thus	*si*
a	*a, sun, un, une*	anger	*corocier, curut, curuz, ire, maltalent*
abandon	*aviler, fuier, fuir, guerpir, laissier*	angry	*iré, irié*
abandoning	*guerpir*	anguish	*l'anguissa*
abjure	*renier, renoier*	announce	*noncier*
about	*converse, conversez, n'en*	answer	*respondre, vus*
above	*seur, sor, soure, sur, sus, suz*	anxiety	*cure*
		any	*nul, nule, rien*
accuse	*apeler*	anyone	*nul*
act	*fet*	anything	*rien*
addressed	*apela*	appeal	*clameor*
advisor	*conseilleor, conseillier*	appearance	*aire, contenant, semblance, semblant*
affair	*cas, chose, cose*		
afflict	*corocier*	appeared	*semblant*
after	*apres, aprés, post, puis*	appreciate	*aviser, prisier, proisier*
afterwards	*apres*	are	*est, estes, sunt*
against	*a, ad, contre, encontre, vers*	arm oneself	*adober*
		army	*maisnie, maisniee*
agree	*acreanter, creanter, granter, otrier, otroier*	arrival	*avenement, venue*
		arrive	*ariver, avenir, parvenir*
agreement	*chartre*	as	*a, com, comme, cum, Si, tant*
a-hundred	*cent*		
all	*pur, tot, tuit, tut, tute, tutes, tuz*	as far as	*jusqu'a*
		ask	*demander, demandez, quere, querre, querrez, requerre, rover*
all that	*quanque*		
allow	*acreanter*		
all-the-day	*tutejur*	ask for	*demander*
alone	*sol*	asked	*demande, demandé*
along	*ala, dales, dallĂŠ, dalles*	asking-for	*querre*
		asks-for	*crie*
a-love	*amez*	as-much	*tant*
already	*ja, jai*	assailed	*asailli*
also	*altresi, aussi*	assault	*eslais*
always	*sempre, sempres*	assemble	*assanler, assembler*
am	*sui*	assured	*aseüré*
a-man	*huem*	as-though	*cum*
among	*entre, mien, nel, od*	astonished	*s'esmerveillent*
amuse	*esbanir*	at	*a, Al*
an	*une*	at once	*ja, jai*
and	*a, e, ed, en, et, si*	attention	*guarde*
		attractive	*avenant*

Word List (English to Old French)

English	*Old French*	English	*Old French*
attractively	*Avenantment*	believed	*creeit, creü*
avenged	*vengiez*	belly	*pance*
avenge-himself	*vengereit*	beloved	*bel, cher*
aware	*aparceüz*	bend	*ploier*
away	*ot*	beseech	*preier, prier, requerre*
		be-taken	*mener*
		betray	*mentir, trair*

B, b

English	*Old French*	English	*Old French*
		betrayed	*traï, traïz*
		better	*mels, miels*
back	*ariere, arire, arrere, arriere*	between	*entre*
bad	*mal, Mals, vilain*	bind	*lier, loier*
badly	*mal, malement*	bird	*oisel*
banned	*ostee*	Bisclavret	*Bisclavret*
baron	*ber*	blast	*alaine, aleine*
barons	*barun, baruns*	blood	*sanc*
battle	*bataille, estor, estorm*	bloody	*sanglent*
be	*aistre, aveir, avoir, d'els, esté, ester, estre, iestre, se faire, seiez*	blow	*empeindre*
		body	*cors*
		bold	*hardi*
be able	*poeir, poier, pooir*	book	*livre*
be accustomed	*soloir*	booty	*eschec*
be afraid	*doter, redoter*	born	*nees*
be dismayed	*esmaier*	brains	*cervel*
be seated	*seoir*	brave	*gentil, hardi*
beak	*bec*	brave knight	*baron*
beard	*barbe*	brave warrior	*baron*
beast	*beste*	bread	*pain*
beaten	*feruz*	break	*fraindre, freindre, rompre*
beautiful	*avenant, bel, gent*		
became	*deveneit, devindrent, devint, fu*	breath	*alaine, aleine*
		Breton	*Bretan*
became-of	*devenuz*	bring	*porter*
because	*car, kar, Pur, quar*	bring before the judge	*presenter*
become	*devenir, deviene*	Brittany	*Bretaigne*
become more painful	*angregier*	brother	*frere*
becomes	*devient*	brought	*aporter, porter*
bed	*lit*	burn	*ardoir, ardre, cuire*
been	*esté, seit*	burst	*rompre*
been-so	*fist*	bush	*buissun*
before	*devant, l'ot, n'ot*	but	*mais, mes, poi, si*
beg	*preier, prier, reclamer*	by	*de, e, Par, pur*
begin	*comencier*	by reason of	*par*
beheld	*tenu*		
behind	*sur*		
behold-this	*ceo*		

C, c

Word List (English to Old French)

English	Old French	English	Old French
cajoled	*blandi*	companions	*cumpaignuns*
call	*apeler, clamer, nomer*	compared with	*contre*
call together	*assanler, assembler*	complain	*plaindre*
call upon	*reclamer, rover*	completely	*tot*
called	*l'apela*	composed	*fez*
came	*vint*	conceal	*celer*
can	*ne, poeir, poeit, poier, pooir*	concealed	*cela*
		concern	*chaloir*
captivity	*prison*	condition	*estre*
capture	*conquerre, cunquerre*	confess	*clamer*
care	*cure*	conquer	*conquerre, cunquerre, veintre*
careful	*curios*		
carry	*porter*	consider	*tenir*
castle	*castel, chastel*	consolation	*consolation*
catapult	*cadable*	conversation	*parlement*
catch	*ataindre*	cook	*cuire*
caught	*l'ourent*	could	*avreie, peüst, poeit, pot, pout, puis*
cause	*engeindre, engendrer*		
chamber	*chambre*	could-have	*pis?*
change	*mut*	could-they	*porent*
chapel	*chapele*	counsel	*cunseil*
character	*figure, moralité*	counselled	*cunseilla*
chase	*Chaciez*	counsellor	*conseilleor, conseillier*
chased	*chaciee, cururent*	count	*conte, conter*
cheating	*engien, engin*	country	*cuntree, païs, regne, terre*
cheese	*fromage*		
chess	*eschecs*	court	*curt*
children	*Enfanz*	courted	*preiee*
christian	*chrestien*	courteous	*curteis*
christian purity	*virginitét*	cowardly	*recreant*
city	*cit, citet*	craft	*art*
clerk	*clerc, clerge*	crazy	*fol*
clever	*cointe, saige, saive*	creature	*chose, cose, ren, rien*
close	*pres, privez*	crimson	*vermeille*
close to	*pres de*	crippled	*enferm*
closed	*ferma*	cross	*trespasser*
clothes	*despueille, dras*	cruel	*dur*
come	*kar, venez, venir*	cry	*plorer*
come out	*issir*	cry out	*escrier*
comes	*vendra*	cut	*trenchier*
comfort	*cunfort*	cut off	*tolir*
coming	*venir*		
commanded	*comandé*	# D, d	
commit	*engagier, mustra*		
commit a crime	*mesprendre*	dame	*dame*
committed	*forfait*		

40

Word List (English to Old French)

English	*Old French*	English	*Old French*
danger	*peril*	distaff	*queloigne, quenoille*
dare	*osasse, oser*	distress	*destresce, ire*
dark	*have*	distressed	*iré, irié*
daughter	*fille*	do	*faire*
day	*di, jor, jorn*	do nothing	*feindre*
days	*jurs*	does	*fait*
day's journey	*jornee*	dogs	*chien, chiens*
days-passed	*Jadis*	doing	*fereit*
dear	*bel*	done	*faire, fait, faites*
death	*mort*	do-not	*nen, n'en*
deceit	*feintise*	doors	*hus*
deceive	*deçoivre, engeignier, engignier*	doubt	*doter, duter, dutez*
		dove	*colomb, colon*
decorative object	*garnement*	draws	*trait*
dedicated	*duné*	dread	*redut*
deep	*altain*	dressed	*aturnez, vestuz*
defeat	*desconfire*	drew-close	*traist*
defense	*garant, garent, resort*	drink	*abevrez, bevre*
deign	*daignier*	dug-out	*cavee*
delay	*demoree, respit*	duke	*duc*
delicious	*delicios*	dwelling	*ostel*
demeanour	*contenant*		
demolish	*desconfire*		
demon	*malfé*		
deny	*mentir, renier, renoier*		

E, e

English	*Old French*
departed	*departi*	earlier	*ainc, ains, ainz*
deprive	*conserrer, consirrer*	earth	*terre*
descend	*descendre*	earthly life	*secle, seule, siecle*
desire	*faim*	eat	*mangier, manjuer*
desired	*requise*	educated	*saige, saive*
destroy	*abatre, perdrai, perir*	eight	*huit*
destruction	*perte*	elegant	*cointe*
devil	*deable, diavle, enemi, malfé*	ell	*alne*
		embraces	*l'acole*
devotion	*servise*	emperor	*empereor*
devour	*devorer*	empty	*vain, vuide, vuit*
devours	*devure*	encountered	*encuntré*
did-he	*s'en*	end	*fenir, finir*
die	*morir*	enemy	*enemi*
difficulty	*destreit*	energy	*element*
direct	*droit*	engaging	*frans*
direction	*sen, sens*	enraged	*enragiez*
disaster	*mal*	entered	*entrerent*
disgrace	*aviler, honte*	entire	*entier, entiers*
dismembered	*depescié*	entirely	*tot*
dismount	*descendre*	escort	*convoier*

Word List (English to Old French)

English	Old French	English	Old French
esteem	*anor, enor, onor, prisier, proisier*	few	*pau, poi, pou*
event	*cas*	fewer	*mains, meins, moins*
ever	*ja, onques*	fief	*anor, chasez, enor, onor*
every	*tot*	fierce	*fier, fort*
everyone	*Ceo*	fifteen	*quinze*
evil	*mal*	find	*trover*
except	*fors, hors*	finery	*parament*
excessively	*trop*	finger	*dei, doi*
exhausted	*mat, recreant*	fire	*feu, fou*
exhort	*enorter*	first	*premiers, primes*
expedition	*chevauchie*	flee from	*fuier, fuir*
expensive	*cher, riche*	flesh	*char, charn*
explaine	*demostrer*	flower	*flor, florir*
expression	*contenant*	fly	*voler*
extremely	*trop*	folding chair for important person	*faldestoed, faldestuef, faldestuel*
eye	*oeuil, oil*	followed	*siwant*
		fondness	*chierté*

F, f

English	Old French	English	Old French
		food	*peüz*
		foot	*pié*
face	*vis, visage*	for	*car, por, pur, quar, que, sa*
face downwards	*adenz*		
facility	*aise*	for a long time	*longement*
fail	*mentir*	for the sake of	*anpur, enpur*
faint	*se pasmer*	forbid	*veer*
fair	*gent*	force	*element*
faith	*fei, foi*	forehead	*temple*
fall	*cas, chaeir, cheoir, perte*	forest	*bois, bos, forest, gualdine*
false		forests	*forez*
false		forget	*ubliër*
family	*feu, fou, lignage, parage*	forgive	*pardoner*
far	*loin, loing, lonc, long, luin*	for-him	*celui*
		form	*figure*
far away	*loin, loing, lonc, luin*	formerly	*ça en arriere*
father	*parent, pere*	for-the-love-of	*s'amur*
favor	*servise*	forward	*avant*
fear	*criem, esfrei, paor, peor, poür, redoter*	found	*trovez*
		found-out	*sot*
feeble	*mat*	frequently	*avenir, sovent*
feed	*paistre, pestre*	friend	*ami, amie, amis*
feel	*sentir*	friendship	*amistié*
feet	*pié*	frightened	*esbai*
felony	*felunie*	from	*de, del*
fence	*escremir, escrimer*	from the direction of	*de vers, devers*

Word List (English to Old French)

English	Old French
from-me	mei
full	plain, plein, ses
full of fervor	balt
full of joy	joieus
furious	enragié, iré, irié
further	mais
furthermore	mes

G, g

English	Old French
game	table
garden	vergier
Garulf	Garulf
gave	duna
generous	riche
gentle	bealz, dolz, dous
gentleman	chevaliers
girl	polle, pucele
girl of noble birth	damoiselle
give	baillier, comander, doner, rendre
give in	concreidre
given	doner
gladly	volentiers
glory	gloire
glove	gant
go	aler, alez, en, met, venir, vois
go away	se departir
go by	trespasser
go out	issir
go to the help of	secorer
god	deu, element
god's	deu
godson	filuel
goes	vait, vet
gold	or
gone	alé, alez
good	ben, bien, bon, bons
good fortune	ben, bien
grace	clementiam, merci, pardon
grand	granz
grandson	neveu, nevot
grant	creanter, durrai, granter, otrei, otrier, otroier
grass	erbre
great	grant, magne
greatly	durement, forment
Greek	gré, gri, grieu, griu
green	vert
greet	saluer
grief	dol, duel, ennui
grow	creistre, croistre
grow worse	angregier
guard	garder, guardent
guarded	guarderent

H, h

English	Old French
ha	ha
had	a, aveit, deüst, fet, fust, la, l'aveit, l'orent, ot, tel, tindrent
had-been	fusse
handsome	Beals, bel, gent
hang	pendre
happen	avenir
happened	avenue, avint, fu, issi
happy	balt, lié, liet, liez
harbour	port
hard	dur, durement, fort
harm	damage, foler, laid, mal, mesfacent, tucha
has	a, l'ait, tel
has-done	fait
has-it	fist
hasten	se hasteier, se haster
hated	haï
hates	het
hatred	haine
hauberk	halberc, osberc
have	ai, aveir, avoir, avrez, tenir
have back	ravoir
have to	devoir
have-we	avum
he	a, cil, el, Ele, en, est, hum, i, Il, le, li, lui, mes, ne, quis, se

Word List (English to Old French)

English	*Old French*	English	*Old French*
head	*chief, teste*	horror	*poür, tristece*
health	*santé*	hour	*eure, ore*
hear	*entendre, odir, Oëz, oir, oïr*	house	*maison, maisun, ostel*
		household	*maisnie, maisniee*
heard	*entendu, oï*	how	*coment, cum, sa*
heart	*coer, cor, cors, cuer, curage*	hunger	*faim*
		hunt	*chacier, chasser*
heathen	*pagien, paien*	hunters	*veneür*
heaven	*ciel*	hurry	*Espleitiez*
he-called	*apela*	husband	*seignur, sire*
he-embraced	*l'acola*		
he-had	*aveit, furent*		
held	*tens, tint*		
hell	*enfern*		

I, i

hello	*ha*	i	*i, jeo, jes, jeu, jo, jol, jou, me*
help	*sucurs*		
he-perceived	*s'aparceit*	i-am	*sui*
her	*la, Le, l'en, li, sis, sun*	i-begin	*m'entremet*
here	*ça, çai, ci, ici, issi*	if	*se, s'en, si*
her-had	*l'aveit*	if-he	*S'il*
he-runs	*curut*	if-him	*s'il*
he-stayed	*herberja*	if-she	*s'el*
he-wanted	*volentiers*	if-some	*s'alcune*
he-was	*esteit*	ignorance	*nonsavoir*
he-went	*ala, alout*	i-hear	*oï*
high	*alt, altain, aut, halt*	i-know	*sai*
hill	*pui*	ill	*enferm*
him	*cil, hum, ki, le, l'en, li, l'i, lui*	illness	*enfermeté, mal*
		immediately	*endreit, maintenant, sempre, sempres, tantost, tost*
him-had	*l'aveit*		
him-loved	*l'amout*		
himself	*meïsmes*	important	*alt, aut, halt*
his	*la, le, les, li, sa, ses, soens, son, sun*	in	*a, ad, Al, as, El, en, sun*
		in front of	*devant*
his-adventure	*s'aventure*	in here	*ceanz, seans*
hit	*fiere*	in order that	*com, cum*
hither	*ça, çai*	in the direction of	*de vers, devers*
hold	*tenir*	in the middle	*par mi, parmi*
hollow	*cruese*	in the midst of	*entre*
holy	*saint*	in the presence of	*devant*
home	*maisun*	in vain	*mar*
homes	*maisun*	indeed	*ja, voir*
honor	*anor, enor, fei, foi, honestét, onor*	indicate	*demostrer*
		indicated	*enseigna*
honored	*honore*	inform	*enseignier*
horn	*cor, corn*	inquired	*enquis*

Word List (English to Old French)

English	*Old French*	English	*Old French*
inside	*dedenz*	knights	*chevaliers*
in-such-way	*cumfaitement*	knock down	*abatre*
intention	*maniere*	know	*apercevoir, savez, savoir*
in-those	*es*		
into	*en*	knowing	*saveit*
invent	*engeignier, engignier*	knowledge	*escïent*
inventory	*livre*	known	*cuneüz, seü*
invoke	*reclamer*	known-him	*veü*
iron	*fer*	knows	*set*
is	*a, en, est, fu, i, la, m'est, s'est*		
is-humbled	*s'umilie*		
island	*ille, isle*		

L, l

English	*Old French*
it	*ce, ceo, ceu, ço, il, la, le, s'en*
it-is	*c'est*
it-seems	*escïent*
i-understand	*j'entent*
ivory horn	*olifant*
i-want	*vueil*
i-wish	*vueil, vus*
I-would-be	*sereie*

English	*Old French*
lady	*dame*
lament	*se dementer*
land	*terre*
large	*grant*
lay	*lais*
lay siege	*asseoir*
lays	*lais*
lead	*deduire, mener*
leave	*congié, cungié, guerpir, laissier, se departir*
led-himself	*cunteneit*
left	*laissier*
leg	*jambe*
legitimate	*leal, loial*
lend	*prester*
less	*mains, meins, moins*
lesson	*moralité*
let	*fai, laissier, les, lur*
letter	*chartre*
let-us	*Alum*
let-us-leave	*laissuns*
liberal art	*art*
lie	*favele, gesir, mentir*
lie down	*couchier, se coucher*
life	*estre*
lift up	*lever*
light	*legier, ligier, loigier*
light-hearted	*legier, ligier, loigier*
likewise	*aussi*
lily	*lil*
lineage	*lignage*
listen	*entent, Oëz*
listen to	*escolter*

J, j

English	*Old French*
jest	*gab*
joy	*joi, joie*
joyful	*lié, liet*
joyous	*joius*
just	*or*

K, k

English	*Old French*
keep	*tenir*
keep from	*astenir*
kill	*morir, ocire*
king	*regem, rei, reis, roi*
kingdom	*regne*
king's	*rei*
kiss	*baisier*
kissed	*baisa*
kisses	*baise*
knew	*saveit, seümes, sout*
knight	*chevalier, chevaliers*

Word List (English to Old French)

English	*Old French*	English	*Old French*
little	*pau, petit, poi, pou*	mass	*masse*
live	*deduire, vif*	matter	*afaire, chaloir*
lived	*maneit*	matting	*nate*
lodge	*herbergier*	me	*jo, me, mei, mes*
long	*loing, lonc, long, longement, lung, lungement*	mean	*mal*
		meat	*char, charn*
		meet	*assanler, assembler, encontrer*
long-after	*lungement*	meeting	*parlement*
look at	*aviser*	melody	*chant*
look for	*quere, querre*	men	*humes*
look-at	*esguardez*	menace	*manace, menace*
loot	*eschec*	mercy	*merci*
lord	*dam, dan, seignor, seignur*	message	*message*
		messenger	*message*
lose	*perdre*	might	*vertu*
loss	*perdre*	mile	*liue, live*
lost	*perdeit, perduz*	mine	*mei*
love	*amer, amor, chier, eim, s'amur*	miracle	*miracle*
		misdeed	*mesfaire*
loved	*amé, amee, amez, amot, chier*	miserable	*chaitif*
		misery	*poverté*
lover	*amant*	misguided	*meserrez*
loyal	*leal, loial*	mislead	*deçoivre*
		missed	*perdeit*

M, m

English	*Old French*	English	*Old French*
		mistake	*colpe, cope, corpe, pechié, tort*
madam	*Dame*	mistreatment	*mesfait*
made	*faire, faiseit*	mistress	*drue*
maiden	*pucele*	money	*argent*
make	*faire, faites*	monk	*moine, monie*
make a mistake	*mesprendre*	more	*mais, mes, plus, plusur, remest*
make known	*reveler*		
makes	*Faites*	most	*Mult, plus*
man	*home, huem, hume, ome*	mother	*mere*
		mountain	*mont, montaigne, pui*
manifest	*apert*	mourn	*plaindre*
manner	*guise*	mouth	*bouche, buche*
many	*asez, assés, bien, maint, meinte, molt, mout, mult, plusur, plusurs, sovent*	much	*Asez, assés, bien, guaires, molt, mout, mult, tel, tres*
many a	*maint*	my	*ma, Mes, mon, mun*
married	*espusee*	my-heart	*cuer*
marry	*esposer*	my-lord	*Sire*
marvel	*merveille*	my-love	*m'amur*
marvellously	*merveille*	myself	*meïsmes*

46

Word List (English to Old French)

English	Old French	English	Old French
		octave	*huitaves*
		of	*a, al, ala, De, del, des, e, ki, la, ot, se*
		of it	*en*

N, n

English	Old French
name	*nom, nomer, non*
naught	*ne*
near	*lez*
neighbours	*veisins*
nephew	*neveu, nevot*
never	*Ja, nonque, unc, unkes*
never-will	*n'i*
next to	*dales, dallĂŠ, dalles*
next to; beside	*delé, deleiz, deles*
next-to	*s'alout*
night	*nuit*
no	*ne, nul, nule*
noble	*debonaire, esteit, gentil*
nobly	*noblement*
noise	*estor, estorm, vois, voiz*
no-longer	*ne*
none	*ne, n'i, nuls*
No-one	*N'i*
nor	*ne, nel, n'en, ni*
Normans	*Norman*
nose	*nes*
noselessly	*esnasees*
noses	*nes*
not	*enne, mie, ne, Nel, nen, n'en, non, nule, pas*
not any	*nul*
not at all	*nïent*
not-at-all	*mie*
not-had	*n'out*
not-has	*n'a*
nothing	*feiz, nïent, rien, rien?*
notice	*apercevoir*
noticed	*l'aperceut*
not-is	*n'est*
now	*Ja, jai, or, ore*
nude	*nuz*

O, o

English	Old French
oath	*sairement*
observe	*viseter*

English	Old French
of noble lineage	*emparenté*
of the king	*regal*
of which	*dont, dunt*
of whom	*dont, dunt*
of-a-man	*d'ume*
offer	*presenter*
of-him	*l'ai, qu'um*
of-one	*d'une*
often	*sovent*
of-the	*ala*
of-them	*des*
of-this	*del*
old	*veil, vieil, viez*
on	*a, ad, en, seur, sor, soure, Sur*
on top of	*en*
once	*onques*
one	*le, om, on, un, Une, uns*
open	*apert*
oppose	*contredire*
opposition	*cuntredit*
or	*o, u*
orchard	*vergier*
order	*comander, rover*
ordered	*mandez*
origin	*parage*
other	*altre*
our	*nostre*
out	*fors, hors*
out of	*hors*
out-of	*de*
outside	*fors*
over	*seur, sor, soure, sur*
overcome	*veintre*
overcome completely	*tresprendre*
overload	*encombrer*
owe	*dei*
own	*baillier, demeine*

P, p

Word List (English to Old French)

English	*Old French*	English	*Old French*
pagan	*pagien, paien*	precisely	*endreit*
page	*bacheler, bachelor*	prepare	*atorner*
pain	*dolor, dolur, enoi, enui*	present	*porofrir, present, presenter*
pardon	*pardoner*	presently	*ore*
parent	*parent*	pretense	*feintise*
part	*part, partez, piece*	previously	*suliëz*
part-with	*partir*	prison	*piere, pierre, prison, serre*
party	*feste*		
pass	*trespasser*	prize	*pris*
path	*chemin, sentier*	proclaim	*clamer*
pay	*prist*	profession	*menestier*
pay attention	*entendre, penser*	promise	*acreanter, fiance*
pay attention to	*escolter*	proper	*droit*
peace	*pes*	prosecute	*asproier*
people	*gent, suens*	protection	*garant, garent*
period	*terme*	protrude	*empeindre*
period of time	*terme, termine*	proud	*fier*
perish	*perdre, perir*	pull	*tirer*
permission	*congié, pardon*	pure	*mer, mier*
permission to leave	*congié*	purposed	*purpensa*
persecution	*empedement*	pursue	*porchacier*
person	*figure, ren, rien*	purveyor	*porveor*
physical or moral weakness	*enfermeté*	put	*feiz, mectre, met, metre, mettre*
piece	*piece*	puts	*met*
pigeon	*colomb, colon*		
pine tree	*pin*		
pity	*merci*		
place	*asseoir, metez*		

Q, q

English	*Old French*
queen	*raine, reine, roine*
queried	*enquis*
questioned	*mise*
questions	*demanda*
quickly	*menu, menut, tost*

English	*Old French*
play	*joer*
please	*plaire*
plunder	*preie*
point out	*enseignier*
poor	*povre*
port	*port*
portion	*part*
poverty	*poverté*
power	*vertu*
powerful	*riche*
praise	*loër*
praised	*losenja*
pray	*orer, preier, prier*
prayer	*oraison, orison, priement*
precious cloth	*paile*
precious object	*parament*

R, r

English	*Old French*
race	*gent*
rage	*rage*
ran	*curut*
rank	*parage*
rather	*ainc, ains, ainz, mais, mels, miels*
reach	*ataindre*
real	*verai*

Word List (English to Old French)

English	*Old French*	English	*Old French*
really	*bien, voirement*	ride	*chevauchie*
reason	*entente, raison, raisun*	right	*droit, endreit*
receive	*baillier*	ring	*anel*
receive as guest	*herbergier*	road	*veie*
receives	*prent*	room	*chambre*
recognize	*aviser, reconoistre*	rooms	*chambres*
recommend	*comander*	rose	*rose*
recounted	*cunta, cunté*	royal	*regal*
re-dress	*reveste*	royal apartment	*chambre*
refined	*cointe*	ruin	*eissil, essil, issil*
refuse	*veer*	run	*corre*
refuse to believe	*mescroire*	running	*curut*
regain	*ataindre*		
regret	*plaindre*		
reject	*geter, giter*		
rejoice	*esleecier*		
relate	*conter*		
released	*descuplé*		
relieved	*guarie*		
remain	*demorer, ester, maindre, remanoir*		
remained	*remest*		
remains	*relef*		
remedy	*resort*		
remember	*resovenir*		
rememberance	*remembrance*		
repair	*refaire*		
repeatedly	*Suventes*		
resign	*conserrer, consirrer*		
resist	*contredire, remanoir*		
respect	*anor, enor, onor*		
responded	*respunt*		
rest	*se reposer*		
restriction	*resort*		
retained	*retenu*		
retain-him	*retenir*		
return	*rendre, retor, retorn, revienc, torner*		
returned	*rendi, rendu, repaira, repairiez, turnez*		
reveal	*reveler*		
revealed	*descovri*		
revolt	*reveler*		
reward	*guerredoner*		
riches	*argent*		
richly	*richement*		

S, s

English	*Old French*
sad	*mat*
sadness	*tristece*
said	*diënt, dist, fait, fet*
salute	*saluer*
savage	*salvage*
saw	*choisi, veïst, vit*
say	*dire*
scraps	*relef*
sea	*mer*
seduce	*engeignier, engignier, enorter*
see	*aviser, veoir*
seek	*porchacier*
seen	*veü*
sees	*veit*
segment	*piece*
seize	*prendre, tenir*
seized	*pris, prist*
sense	*sen, sens*
sent-for	*manda*
servant	*pucele, servant*
serve	*servir*
served	*servir*
service	*menestier, servise*
set	*mise*
set up	*asseoir*
seven	*set*
several	*pluisor, plusor*
shame	*honte, hunte*
she	*el, ele, li, se*

Word List (English to Old French)

English	*Old French*	English	*Old French*
shed tears	*plorer*	soul	*alme, ame, anima, anme, arme*
she-dressed	*s'apareillot*	sound	*soner, suner*
shelter	*herbergier*	speak	*parler*
she-sent-for	*l'enveia*	speech	*oraison, orison, parole, raison*
she-was-terrified	*s'esfrea*	spin	*filer*
shield	*escu*	spiritual purity	*virginitét*
ship	*nef*	staircase	*degré*
should	*devez*	stake	*ré, rei, rez*
shout	*braire, crier, escrier*	stand	*ester, estut*
show	*demostrer, mener*	standard bearer	*gunfanuner*
shy away	*feindre*	standing	*estait*
sick	*have*	start	*comencier*
sides	*parz*	stay	*demoree, demorer, maindre, remanoir*
sight	*ses*	stayed	*esteit*
silver	*argent*	stick	*verge*
simple bed	*grabatum*	still	*encor, encore, uncore*
sin	*colpe, cope, corpe, pechié*	stirrup	*estrié*
since	*puis*	stomach	*pance*
sing	*braire, chanter*	stone	*piere, pierre*
sir	*dam, dan*	stop	*fenir, finir*
sire	*Sire*	story	*favele*
sires	*Seignur*	straight	*dreit*
sit	*seoir*	street	*rue*
skill	*engien, engin*	strength	*vertu*
sleep	*som, some*	striving	*travailliez*
sleeping	*dormant*	strong	*alt, aut, fier, fort, halt, riche*
slept	*culchier*	study	*estude, estudie*
small	*petit*	subsequently	*end, ent, puis*
smash to pieces	*pecier*	such	*cele, ceo, tant, tel*
smell	*sentir*	such-time	*tant*
snatched	*esracha*	suffer	*pener*
so	*dunc, fu, Issi, si, Tant, vis*	suffering	*dol, dolor, duel, paine, peine*
so much	*tant*	summon	*apeler*
somber	*have*	supple	*legier, ligier, loigier*
some	*alkun, aucun*	support	*sostenir*
somebody	*alme, ame, anme, arme*	sure	*seur, sur*
somehow	*coment*	surprised	*esbai*
so-much	*tant*	suspect	*mescroire*
son	*fil, filuel*	sustain	*sostenir*
song	*chant*	sweet	*debonaire, dolz, dous, dulz*
soon	*maintenant, tost*	swift	*hastif*
sorely	*durement*		
sorrowful	*dolent*		
sought-for	*demandez*		

Word List (English to Old French)

English	Old French	English	Old French
swoon	se pasmer	theft	ravine
sword	espee	their	leur, lor, lur
		the-king	rei
		the-knight	chevalier

T, t

English	Old French	English	Old French
		the-last	Cist
		the-morning	demain
table	table	then	a, donc, en, puis, s'en, unt
take	mener, prendre		
take hold of	prendre	the-name	nun
take off	tolir	the-one	Cil
take-care	guardez	the-other	l'altre
taken-aside	prise	the-palace	palais
taken-away	toli	there	i, ilec, iluec, iluoc, La, l'en, vet
takes	meine		
talk	parler	therefore	donc, Kar, Pur
tall	grant	these	cez
task	servise	the-story	L'aventure
teach	enseignier	the-time	piece
tear	deciré	the-wife	femme
teeth	denz	they	Cil, il, l'unt, sunt, unt
tell	di, dire, dis, dist, dites, noncier	they-call	l'apelent
		they-find	truevent
tells	direit	they-had	eüz
temple	temple	they-live	viveient
tenderly	tendrement	they-were	sunt
term	terme	they-would-have	l'eüssent
territory	chambre	thick	espés
than	de, que	thing	chose, cose, ren, rien
thanks	mercie	think	cuidier, penser
that	a, ce, cele, ceo, ceu, cil, ço, e, est, ki, la, l'a, qu'a, que, qui, qu'il, tant	thirty four	trente et quatre
		this	ce, cele, ceo, Cest, ceste, ceu, cist, ço, euc, Iceste, l'a, le, li, o, ou, sa
that much	si		
that way	si		
that-day	jur	this-day	hui
that-heard	l'oï	this-he	Cil
that-in	qu'en	those	cels
that-one	celui	thought	quidot
that-time	cele	thought-they	quidouent
the	al, as, cel, la, le, les, li	thousand	millier
the-adventure	l'aventure	threatened	manaça, manacié
the-beast	beste	three	trei, treis, trois
the-clothing	despueille	throne	faldestoed, faldestuef, faldestuel
the-country	païs		
the-end	chief	through	par, par mi, parmi
the-event	l'aventure	throw	geter, giter

Word List (English to Old French)

English	*Old French*	English	*Old French*
thus	*Issi, si, s'i*	trouble	*damage, guerre*
time	*eure, feiz, ore, tans, tens, veiz*	troubled	*esbai*
		true	*verai*
times	*feiz*	true	*veraie*
time-to-time	*sovent*	true	*veritez*
title	*nom, non*	true	*voir*
to	*a, ad, al, de, del, en, encontre, se, seur, sor, soure, sur, vers*	truly	*voir*
		try	*entendre*
		tumult	*estor, estorm*
to-ask	*demandasse*	turn	*atorner, torner*
to-be	*seit*	two	*Dous*
to-bite	*mordre*		
today	*oi, ue, ui*		
to-embrace	*enbracier*		
together	*comunalment, ensemble*		

U, u

English	*Old French*
together with	*ensemble od*
to-go	*errer*
to-help	*aidier*
to-him	*ariere, li*
to-lie	*gisir*
to-lose	*perduz*
to-me	*me, mei, m'en, Mun*
too much	*trop*
took	*mena, menez, pris, toluz*
to-part	*partir*
to-recount	*cunter*
torment	*asproier, enoi, enui, paine, peine*
torture	*pener*
to-separate	*desevrer*
to-talk-with	*parler*
totally	*tuz*
to-the	*al, la*
tourney	*tornoier*
toward	*vers*
towards	*encontre, envers, vers*
tower	*tor*
town	*cit, citet*
travelled	*tint*
travels	*tint*
treated	*bailliz, mis*
tree	*bois, bos*
tremble	*trembler*
troops	*compaigne*

English	*Old French*
ugly	*vilain*
under	*a, desos, desous, sos, soz, suz*
under-pressed	*suzprist*
understand	*entendre*
understanding	*sages*
unhappy person	*entrepris*
unhealthy	*enferm*
unrefined	*dur*
until	*desi, tant, tresqu', trusqu'*
until now	*ça en arriere*
unto	*En*
up	*sus, suz*
up to	*a, ad, jusqu'a, tresqu', trusqu'*
urge	*enorter*
us	*nus*
used	*suleit*
utter	*geter, giter, soner, suner*

V, v

English	*Old French*
valiant	*vaillant*
vanquish	*veintre*
various	*divers*
very	*durement, forment, molt, mout, Mult, tres*
very much	*forment*
very well	*asez, assés*

Word List (English to Old French)

English	*Old French*	English	*Old French*
very-important	*munte*	which	*dunt, ki, qu'avez, que, quel, qu'il*
very-well	*bonement, tresbien*		
village	*rue*	which-of	*qu'il*
virgin	*virge*	which-that	*qu'il*
visible	*aparant, apert*	whirl around	*tornoier*
visit	*viseter*	white	*blanc*
voice	*vois, voiz*	who	*ki, le, que, qui, s'en*
		who-here	*qu'ici*

W, w

		who-him	*celui*
		whole	*tot*
		whose	*dont, dunt*
wall	*mur*	wide	*lee*
want	*quere, querre, voloir, vueil, vueille*	wife	*espuse, femme*
		wild rose	*aiglantier, aiglent*
wanted	*voleit, volt*	will-do	*ferez*
wants	*volt*	willed	*volt*
war	*guerre*	will-hunt	*chacerai*
war cry	*enseigne*	willing	*volentiers*
was	*a, ert, est, esté, ester, fu, fust, li, s'en*	will-part	*partirai*
		will-tell	*dirai*
was-he	*esteit*	wine	*vin*
watch over	*garder*	wise	*sages*
way	*guise, maniere, veie*	with	*atot, avec, avoc, avuec, cum, de, en, ensemble, i, mes, o, od, of, ot, qu'el*
way of life	*estre*		
ways	*endreit*		
we	*nos, nus*		
weak	*enferm, vain*	with-a	*d'une*
weapon	*fer*	without	*senz*
wear	*porter*	woman	*dame, Femme*
weather	*tans, tens*	women	*femmes*
week	*semeine*	wonder	*merveille*
well	*bel, bien*	wonders	*merveille*
well-being	*ben, bien, santé*	woods	*boscages*
went	*ala, alez, alout, repairié, vait, vers*	word	*mot, parlement, parole, raison, vois, voiz*
were	*eüsse, furent*	world	*mund, secle, seule, siecle*
werewolf	*Bisclavret*		
wetched	*dolent*	worse	*peüst*
we-will-see	*verruns*	worship	*adurer*
what	*cument, que, quei, quel, qu'est, qui, qu'il*	worthy-man	*prozdum*
		would	*deüst*
what is surprising	*merveille*	would-be	*fussent*
what-have	*Qu'ai*	would-have	*eüst*
when	*com, comme, Quant, que*	would-look-like	*semblereit*
		wretched	*mal*
where	*ou, u*	wretchedness	*eissil, essil, issil*
whether	*s'il, U*		

Word List (English to Old French)

English	Old French
wrongly	*mar*

Y, y

year	*an*
yet	*encor, encore, si, uncore*
yield	*ploier*
you	*die, Ne, tu, vos, vus*
you-have	*vus*
you-heard	*oïe*
young knight aspirant	*bacheler, bachelor*
young man	*bacheler, bachelor*
your	*tes, ton, vostre, voz, vus*
yours	*vus*
you-see	*vei*

Z, z

zeal	*estude, estudie*

www.ingramcontent.com/pod-product-compliance
Lightning Source LLC
Chambersburg PA
CBHW051424070526
44584CB00023B/3569